Bradley's NEW TASTE OF THE BEST!

A Potpourri of Musical Styles!

Arranged by
RICHARD BRADLEY

Also Sprach Zarathustra — Richard Strauss	70
Amazing Grace	48
Ashokan Farewell (from "The Civil War")	58
The Battle Hymn Of The Republic	46
Beverly Hills, 90210	54
Can't Let Go	10
Canon In D — Johann Pachelbel	76
Chariots Of Fire	32
Clair de Lune (First Theme) — Claude Debussy	72
Embraceable You	92
The Entertainer (used in "The Sting")	38
Fairest Lord Jesus	51
Funeral March Of The Marionettes (Theme from "Alfred Hitchcock Presents")	62
Für Elise (Main Theme) — Ludwig van Beethoven	74
Get Here	19
(Everything I Do) I Do It For You (from "Robin Hood: Prince Of Thieves")	27
L.A. Law (Main Title)	64
Lullaby Of Birdland	83
The Man I Love	89
Misty	80
Moonlighting	60
Oh Happy Day	44
Save The Best For Last	2
Saving All My Love For You	22
Someone To Watch Over Me	86
Sometimes Love Just Ain't Enough	14
The Sorcerer's Apprentice — Paul Dukas	67
Star Wars (Main Title)	41
Strike Up The Band	94
The Summer Knows (Theme from "Summer Of '42")	35
What A Friend We Have In Jesus	52
The Wind Beneath My Wings	6

ISBN 0-89898-911-6

Copyright © 1989, 1994 BRADLEY PUBLICATIONS
All Rights Assigned to and Controlled by CPP/BELWIN, INC.
15800 N.W. 48th Avenue, Miami, FL 33014

WARNING: Any duplication, adaptation or arrangement of the compositions contained in this collection, without the written consent of the owner, is an infringement of U.S. copyright law and subject to the penalties and liabilities provided therein.

Bradley Publications
a division of
RBR Communications, Inc.

CPP Belwin, Inc.

Save The Best For Last

Words and Music by
WENDY WALDMAN, JON LIND
and PHIL GALDSTON
Arranged by Richard Bradley

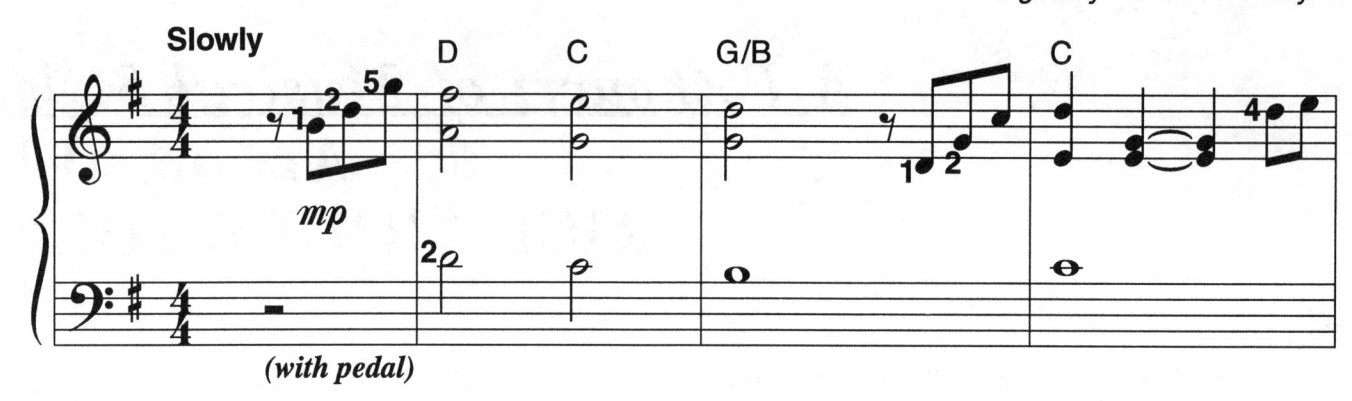

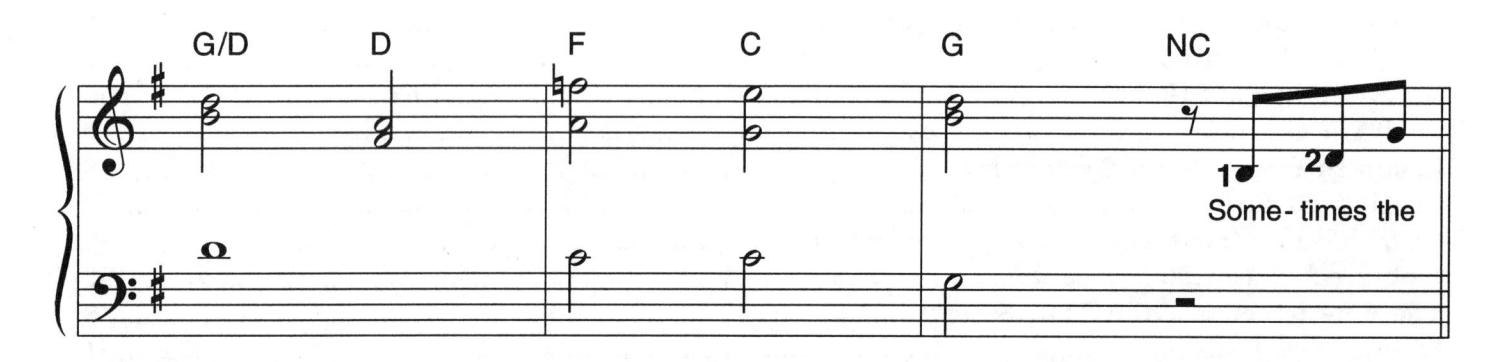

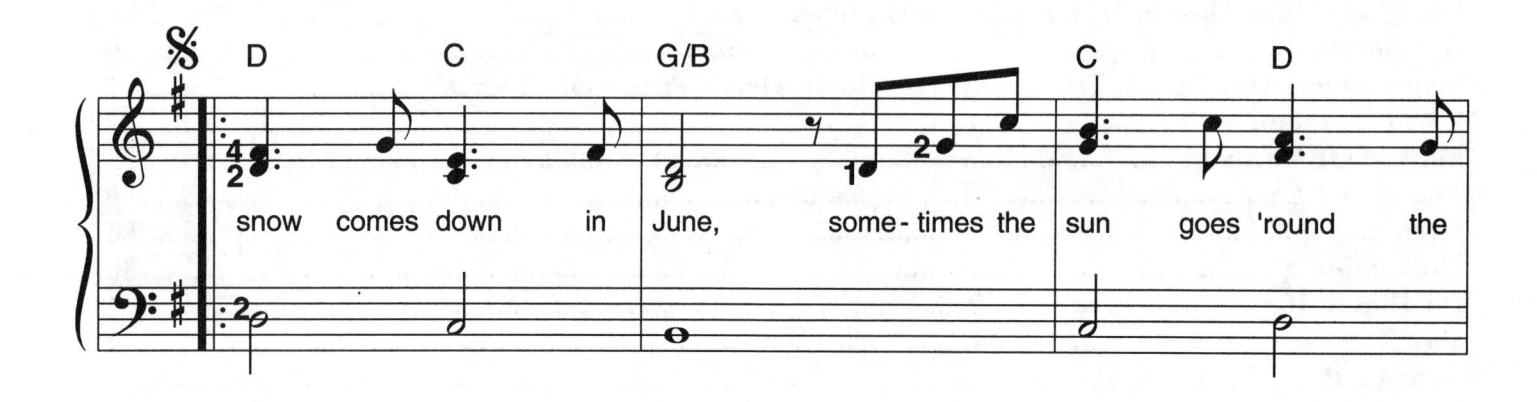

Slowly

mp

(with pedal)

Some- times the snow comes down in June, some- times the sun goes 'round the moon. I see the pas- sion in your eyes, some- times it's

Save The Best For Last - 4 - 1

© 1989, 1992 WINDSWEPT PACIFIC ENTERTAINMENT Co.
d/b/a LONGITUDE MUSIC CO., MOON AND STARS MUSIC,
POLYGRAM INTERNATIONAL PUBLISHING, INC., KAZZOOM MUSIC, INC., VIRGIN SONGS, INC.
Rights on behalf of MOON AND STARS MUSIC administered by WINDSWEPT PACIFIC
Rights for BIG MYSTIC MUSIC controlled and administered by VIRGIN SONGS, INC.
All Rights Reserved

To Coda
C D G C
all a big sur - prise. 'Cause there was a time when all I
G/B Am7 D7 G
did was wish you'd tell me this was love. It's not the
Dm7 C/E F C/E
way I hoped, or how I planned, but some - how it's e -
D7 NC D C G/B
nough. And now we're stand - ing face to face, is - n't this

world a cra-zy place? Just when I thought our chance had passed, you go and save the best for last.

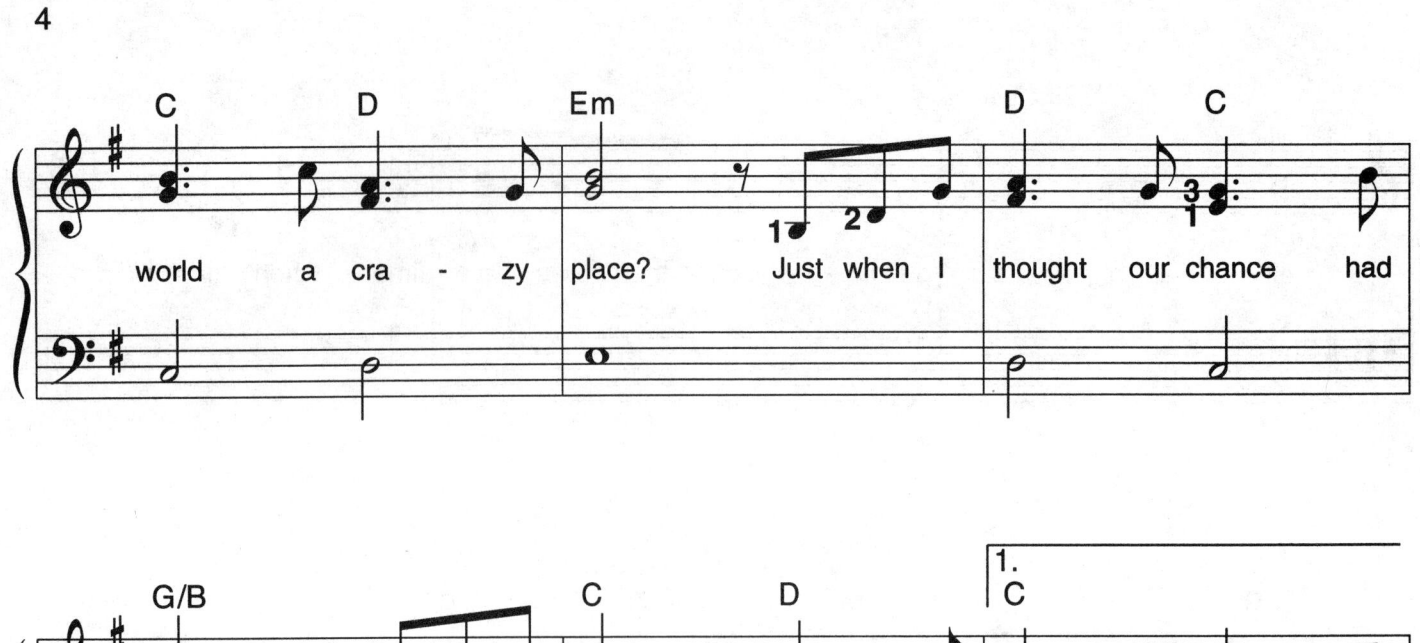

All of the last. Some-times the ver-y thing you're look-ing for is the

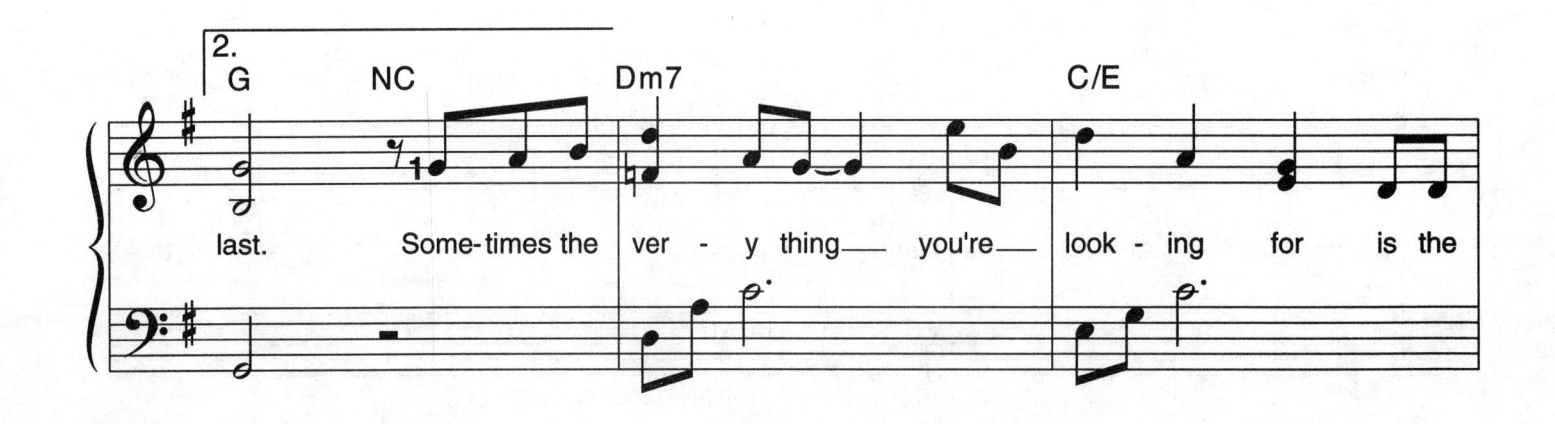

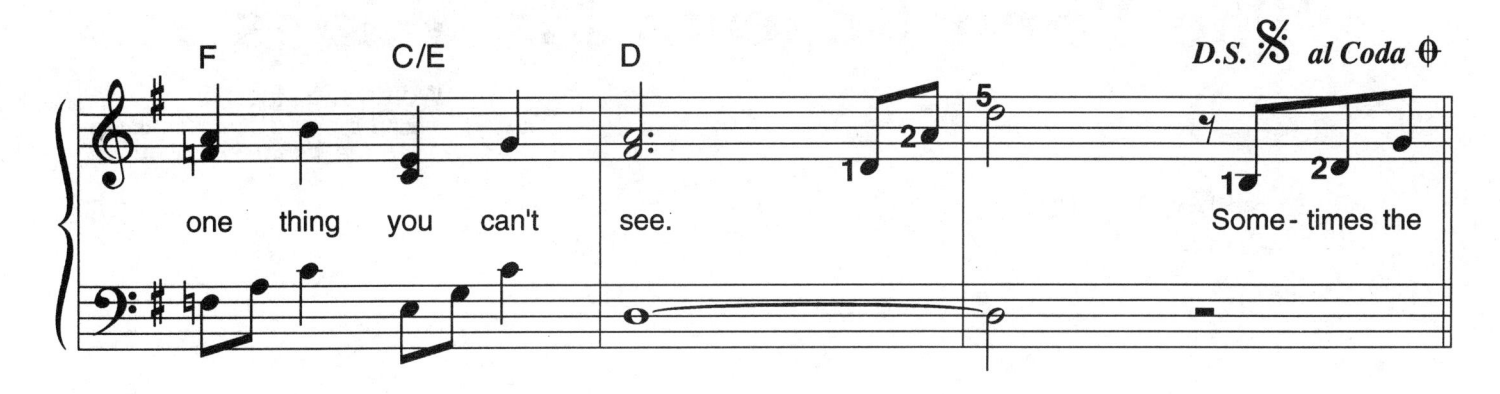

Verse 2:
All of the nights you came to me
When some silly girl had set you free.
You wondered how you'd make it through,
I wondered what was wrong with you.
'Cause how could you give your love to someone else
And share your dreams with me?
Sometimes the very thing you're looking for
Is the one thing you can't see.

Verse 3:
Sometimes the snow comes down in June,
Sometimes the sun goes 'round the moon.
Just when I thought our chance had passed,
You go and save the best for last.

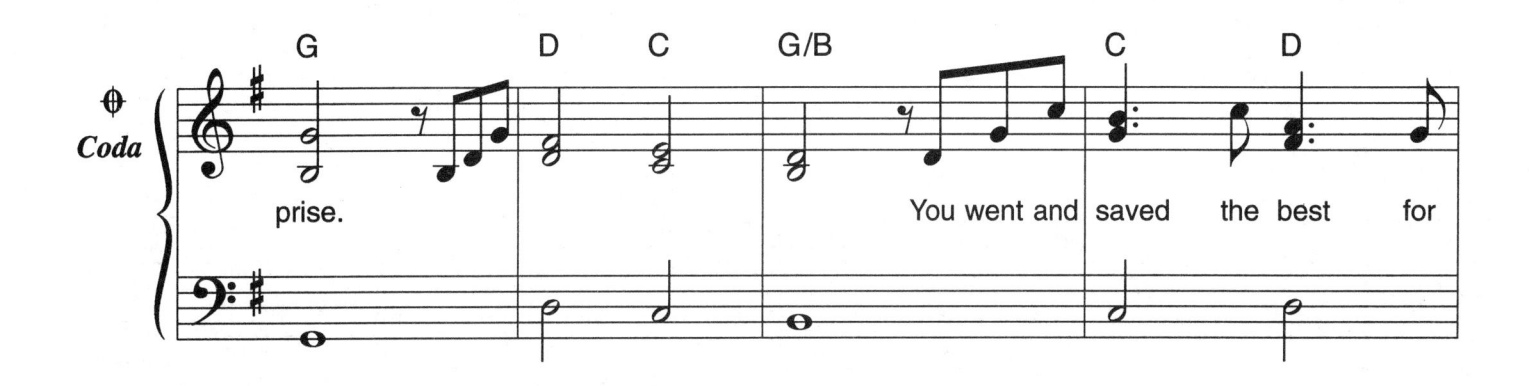

The Wind Beneath My Wings

Words and Music by
LARRY HENLEY and JEFF SILBAR
Arranged by Richard Bradley

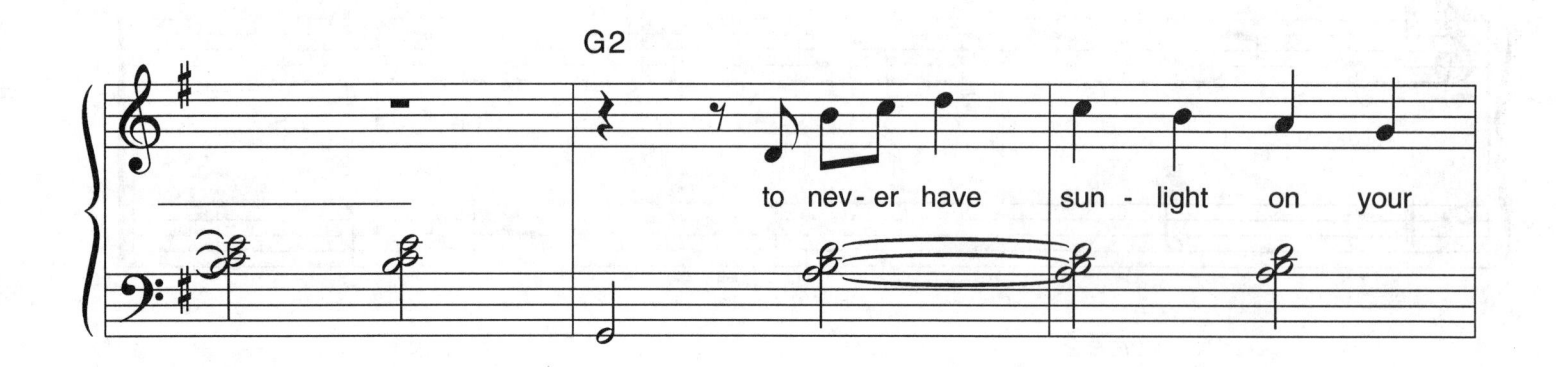

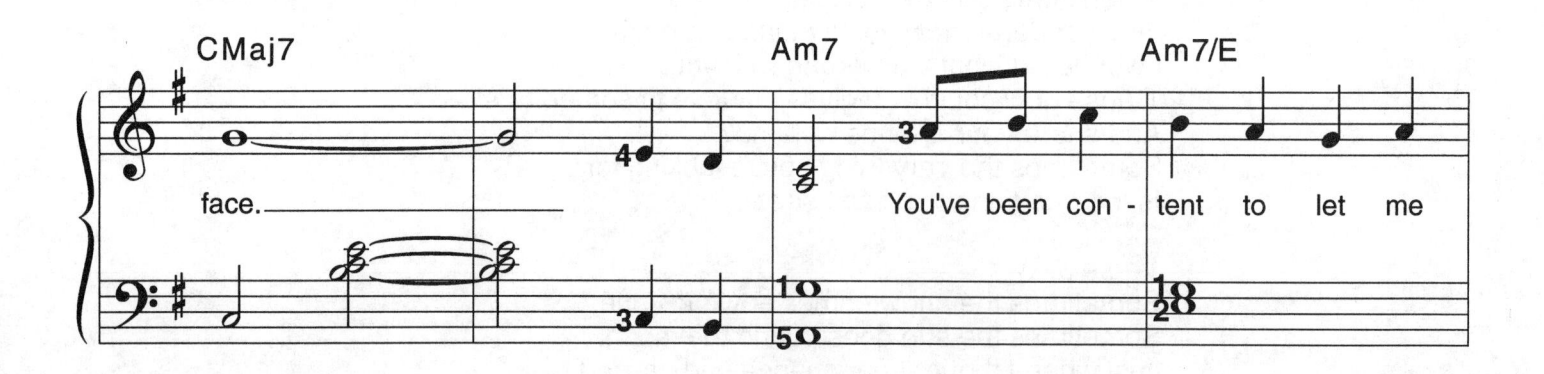

Slowly, flowing

It must have been cold there in my shadow, to never have sunlight on your face. You've been content to let me

The Wind Beneath My Wings - 4 - 1

© 1982, 1986 WARNER HOUSE OF MUSIC & WB GOLD MUSIC CORP.
All Rights Reserved

D7sus D7 Am7 Am7/E
shine, you al - ways walked the step be -
1. D7sus D7
hind.
2.3. D7sus D7 B7
plain.
Em NC G
Did you ev - er know that you're my he - ro,
D/F♯ Em NC
and ev - 'ry - thing I'd like to

G D/F♯ Em D C NC
be? I can fly
G D/F♯ Em D
high - er than an ea - - - - gle
Am7 NC To Coda Am D7 G2
'cause you are the wind be - neath my wings.
CMaj7
D.S. al Coda

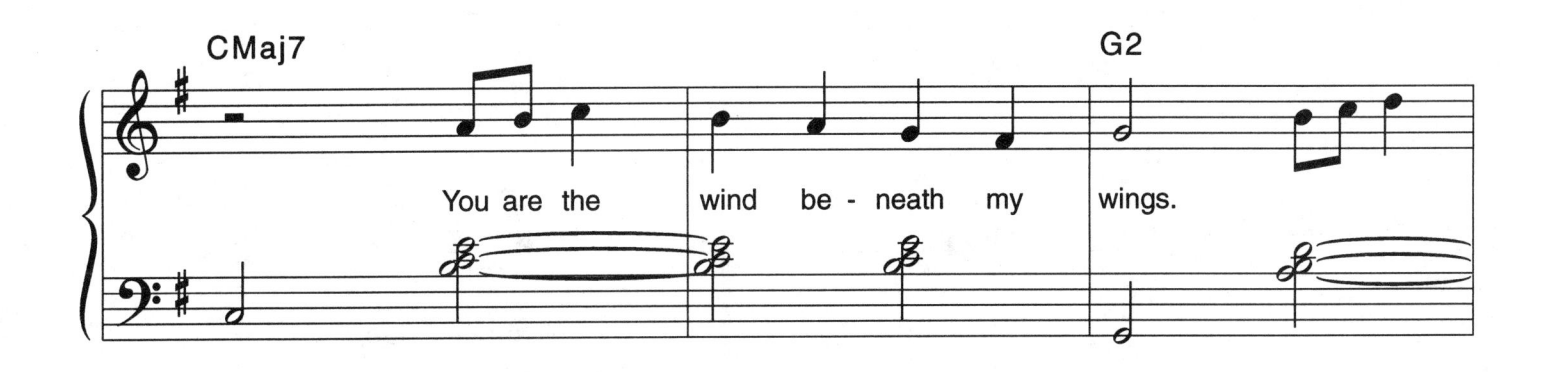

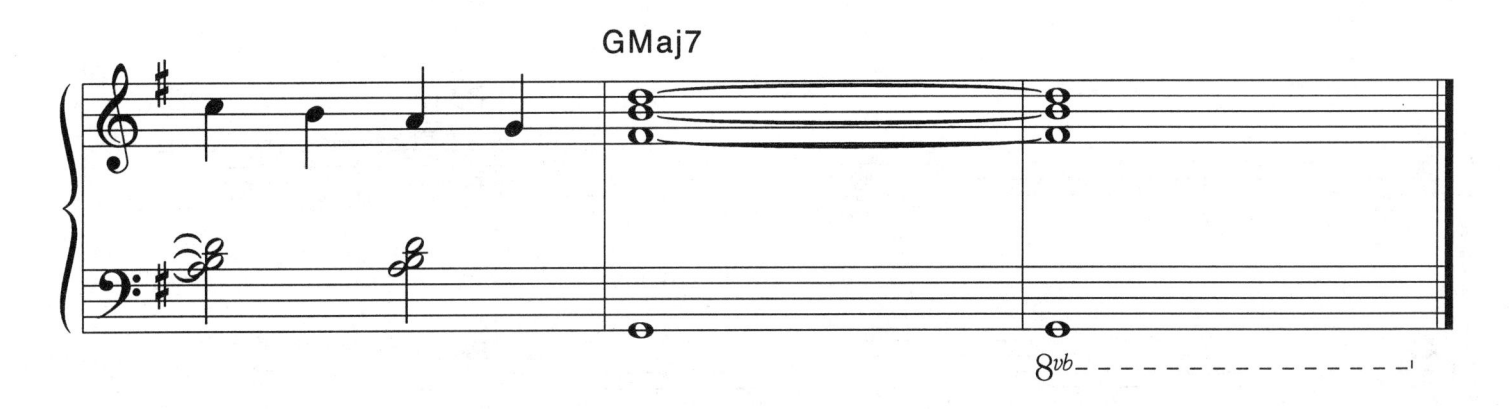

Verse 2:
I was the one with all the glory
While you were the one with all the strength,
Only a face without a name,
I never once heard you complain.

Verse 3:
It might have appeared to go unnoticed
That I've got it all here in my heart.
I want you to know the truth
I would be nothin' without you.

Can't Let Go

Words by
MARIAH CAREY

Muisc by
WALTER AFANASIEFF and MARIAH CAREY
Arranged by Richard Bradley

There you are, holding her hand. I am lost, dying to understand. Didn't I cherish you right? Don't you know

Can't Let Go - 4 - 1

© 1991, 1992 WB MUSIC CORP., WALLYWORLD MUSIC, SONY SONGS INC. and MARIAH CAREY SONGS
All rights on behalf of WALLYWORLD MUSIC administered by WB MUSIC CORP.
Rights for SONY SONGS INC and MARIAH CAREY SONGS administered by SONY MUSIC PUBLISHING
All Rights Reserved

B♭/D
NC
you were my life?
E - ven though I
D♭Maj7
E♭
F
D♭Maj7
E♭
try, I can't let go.
Some - thing in your eyes cap - tured my
F
D♭Maj7
E♭
soul.
And ev - 'ry night I see you in my
F
To Coda
D♭Maj7
E♭
1.
F
dreams.
You're all I know. I can't let go.
Just

2.
F Fm C
go. Do you e - ven re - a - lize the
Ab/Eb Bb/D DbMaj7
sor - row I have in - side ev - 'ry day of my
C7sus C7 Fm C/E
life? Do you know the way it feels when
Ab/Eb Bb/D DbMaj7
all you have just dies? I try and try to de -

Verse 2:
Just cast aside,
You don't even know I'm alive.
You just walk on by,
Don't care to see me cry.
Here I am, still holding on.
I can't accept my world is gone.
(Chorus)

Sometimes Love Just Ain't Enough

Words and Music by
GLEN BURTNICK and PATTY SMYTH
Arranged by Richard Bradley

Slowly

2. nough.

(with pedal)

Now I don't wan-na lose you, but I don't wan-na use you
Now I could nev-er change you, I don't wan-na blame you,

just to have some-bod-y by my side.
ba-by, you don't have to take a fall.

And I don't wan-na hate you, I don't wan-na take you,
Yes, I may have hurt you, but I did not de-sert you,

Sometimes Love Just Ain't Enough - 5 - 1

© 1992 EMI BLACKWOOD MUSIC INC., PINK SMOKE MUSIC, WB MUSIC CORP. and BMG SONGS, INC.
All rights for PINK SMOKE MUSIC controlled and administered by EMI BLACKWOOD MUSIC INC.
All Rights Reserved

E♭
F
but I don't wan - na be the
one to cry.
may - be I just wan - na
have it all.
B♭
F
Am7
B♭
And that don't real - ly mat - ter
to an - y one an - y
It makes a sound like thun - der,
it makes me feel like
F
Am7
B♭
Am7
more.
But like a fool I keep
los - in' my place, and I keep
rain.
And like a fool who will
nev - er see the truth, I keep
C
Dm7
C/E
see - in' you walk through that door.
But there's a
think - in' some - thing's gon - na change.

B♭ F C F
dan - ger in lov - in' some-bod - y too much, and it's
B♭ F C F
sad when you know it's your heart you can't trust. There's a
they can't touch.
B♭ F C Dm7
To Coda
rea - son why peo - ple don't stay where they are, ba - by,
who
1. 2.
B♭ C B♭ C F
some-times love just ain't e - some-times love just ain't e - nough. And there's

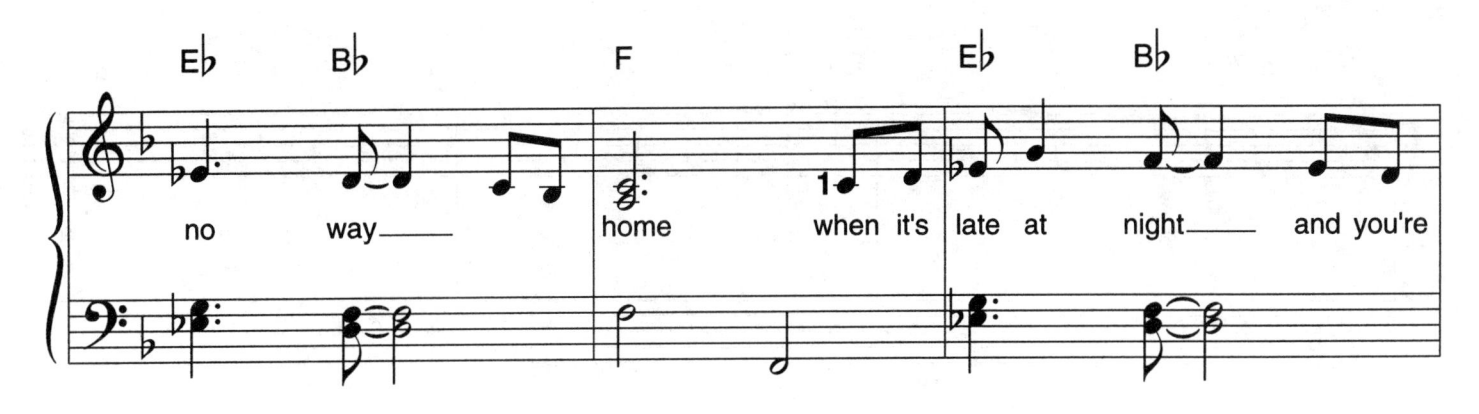

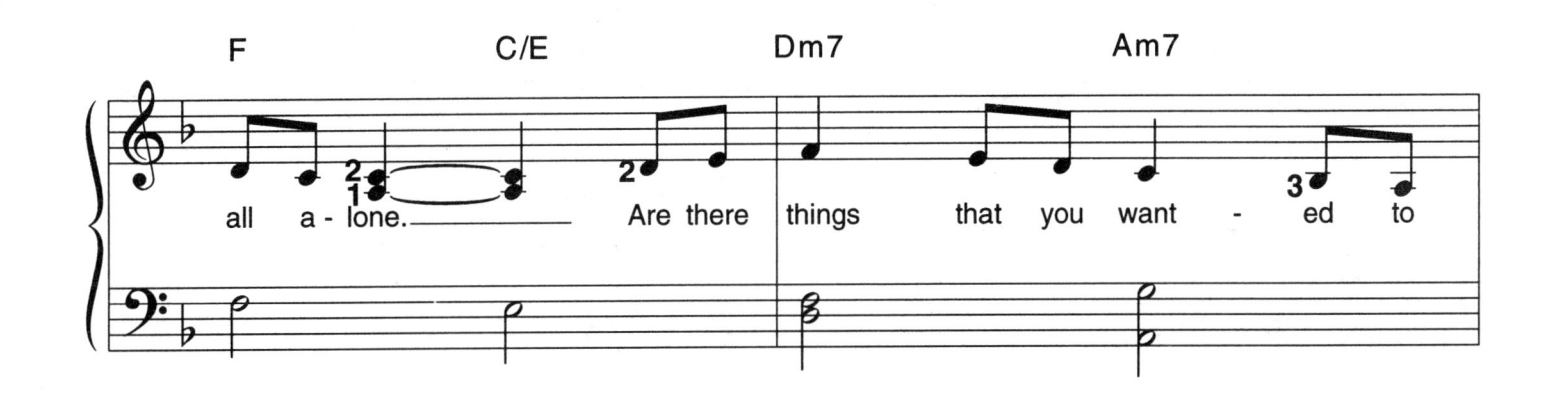

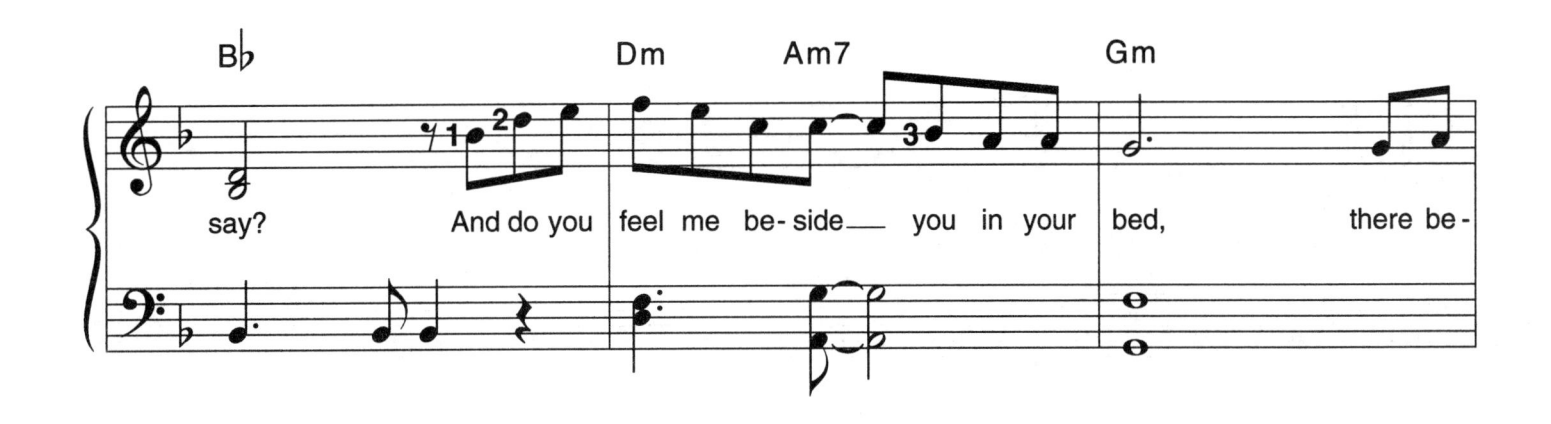

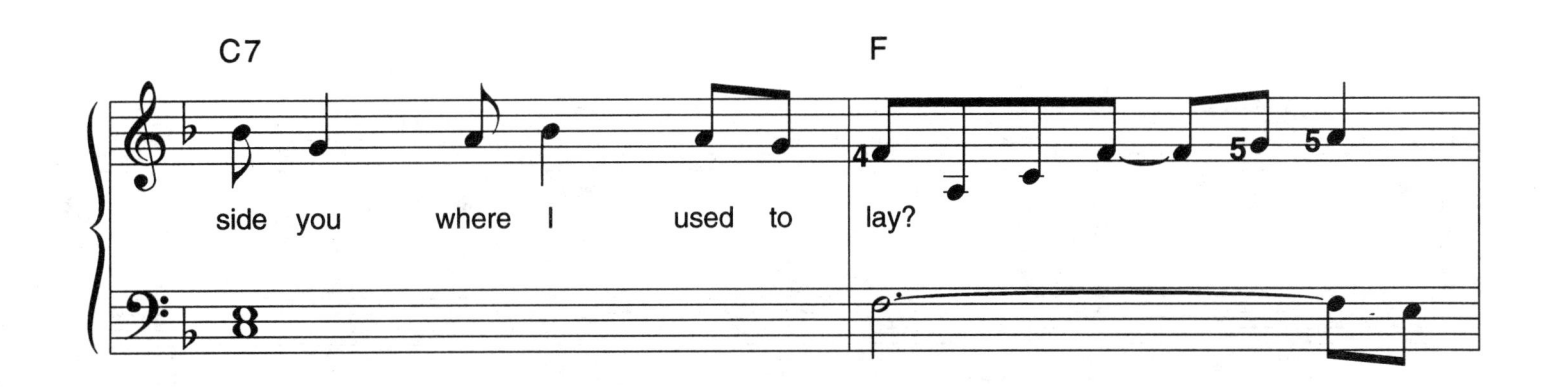

no way— home when it's late at night— and you're all a-lone.— Are there things that you want-ed to say? And do you feel me be-side— you in your bed, there be-side you where I used to lay?

Dm7
E♭
F
D.S. 𝄋 al Coda 𝄌
And there's a
𝄌 Coda
B♭
C
Dm7
some - times love just ain't e - nough. Ba - by,
B♭
B♭/D
C
F
some times love, it just ain't e - nough.
Dm
E♭
F

Get Here

Words and Music by
BRENDA RUSSELL
Arranged by Richard Bradley

Lyrics:

You can reach me by car-a-van, cross the des-ert like an A-rab man. I don't care how you get here, just get here if you can.

You can reach me by can. There are hills and moun-tains be-tween us, al-ways some-thing to get o-ver.

Verse 2:
You can reach me by sailboat,
Climb a tree and swing rope to rope.
Take a sled and slide down slope
Into these arms of mine.
You can jump on a speedy colt,
Cross the border in a blaze of hope.
I don't care how you get here,
Just get here if you can.

Verse 3:
You can windsurf into my life,
Take me up on a carpet ride.
You can make it in a big balloon
But you better make it soon.
You can reach me by caravan,
Cross the desert like an Arab man.
I don't care how you get here,
Just get here if you can.

Saving All My Love For You

Words by
GERRY GOFFIN

Music by
MICHAEL MASSER
Arranged by Richard Bradley

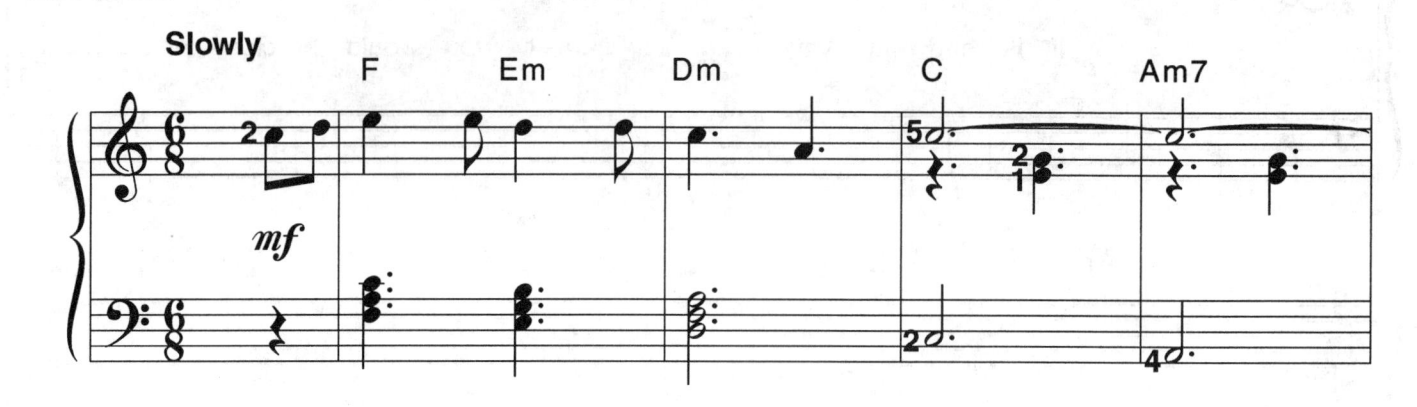

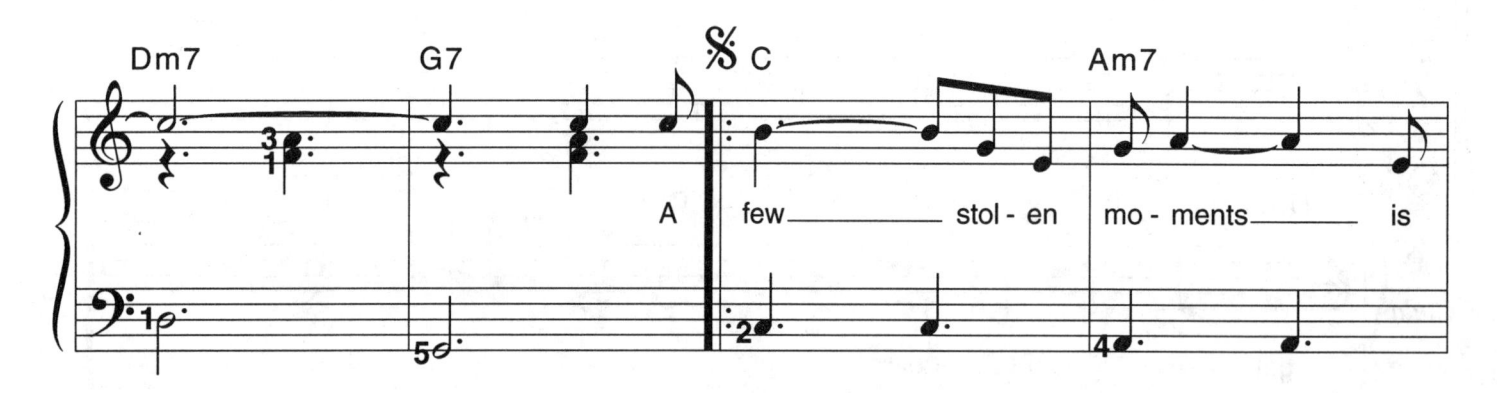

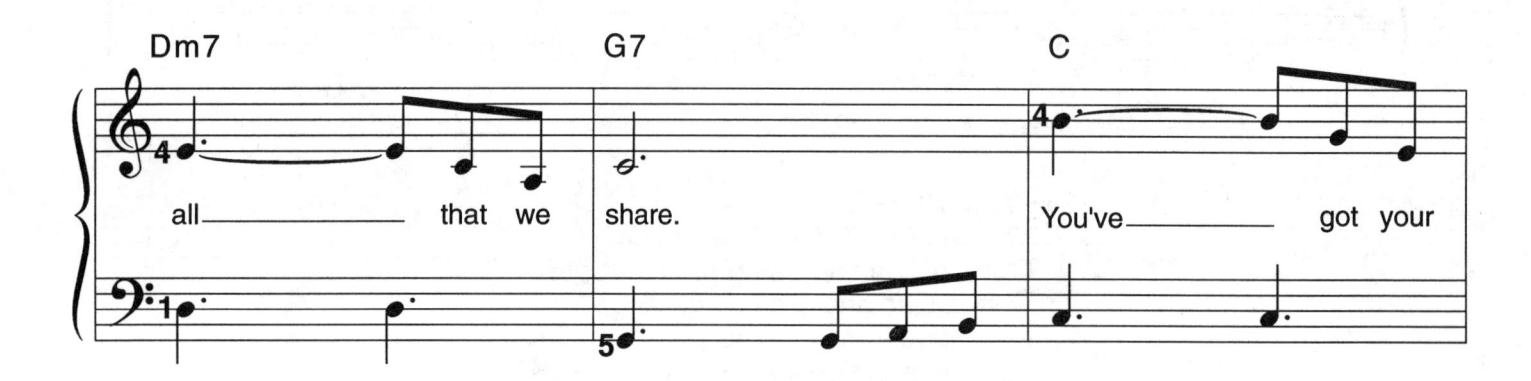

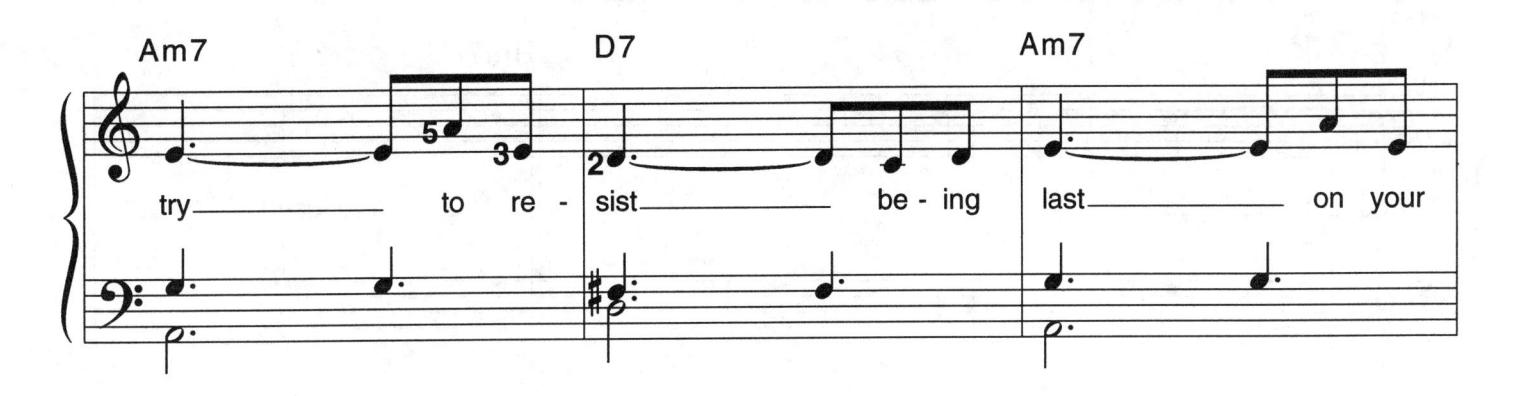

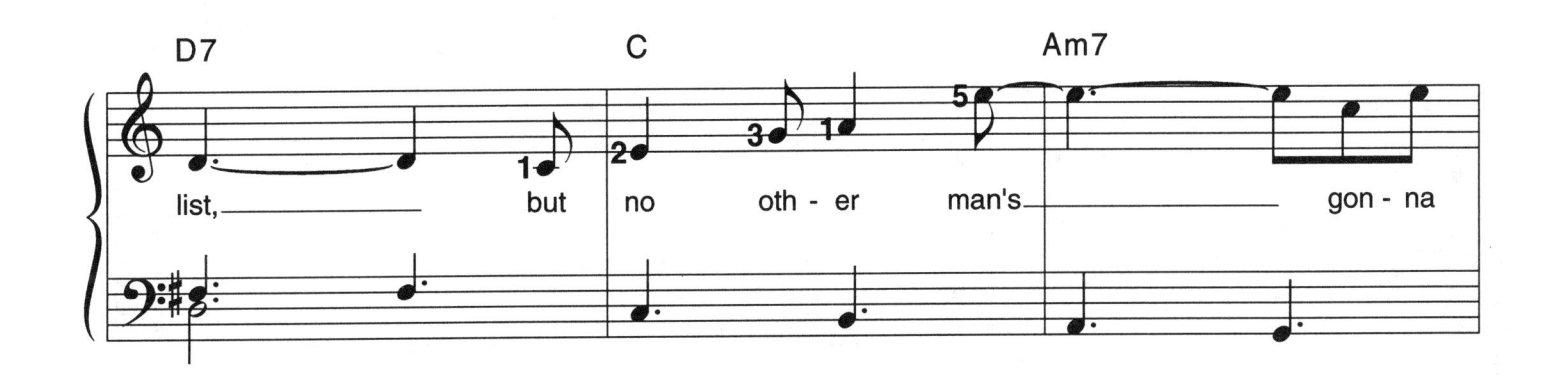

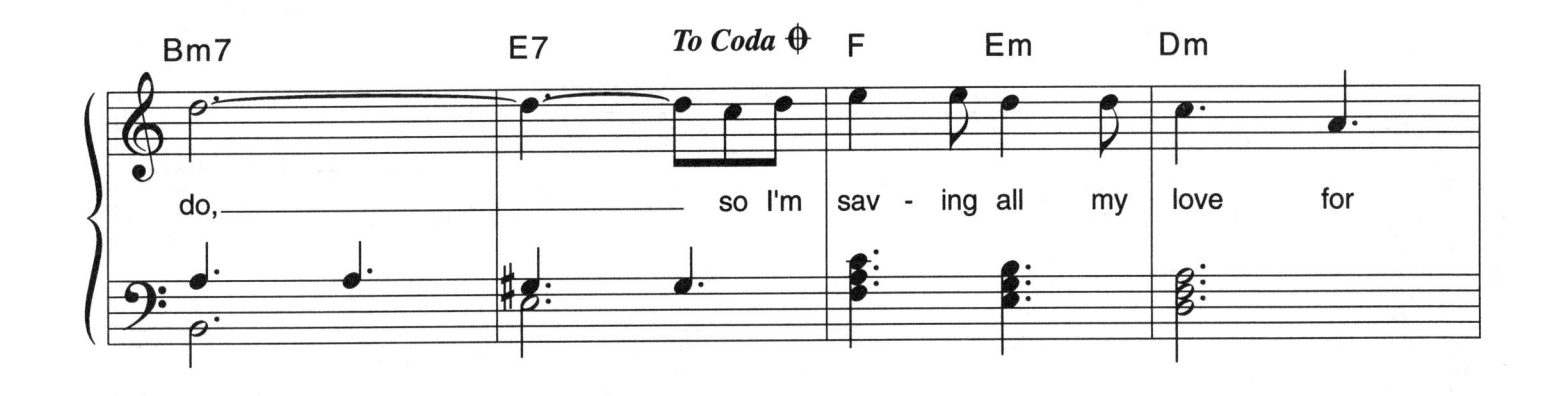

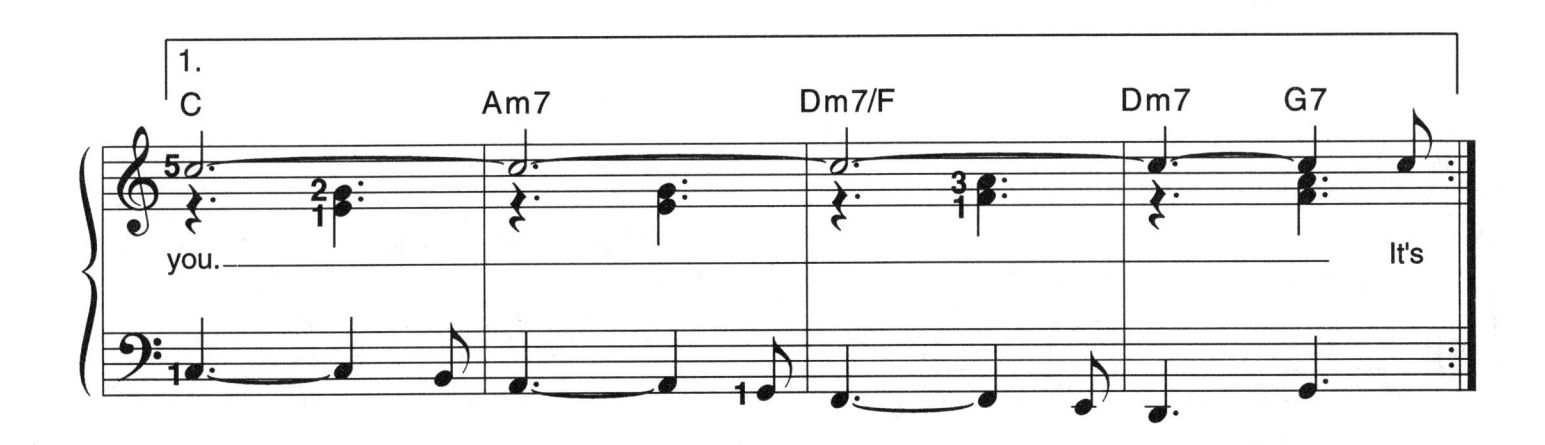

Saving All My Love For You - 5 - 2

2.
C
Bm7
you.
You used to
E
Am7
tell me we'd run a - way to - geth - er;
Dm7
G7
CMaj7
love gives you the right to be free.
C6
F♯m7
B7
You said: "Be pa - tient, just

25

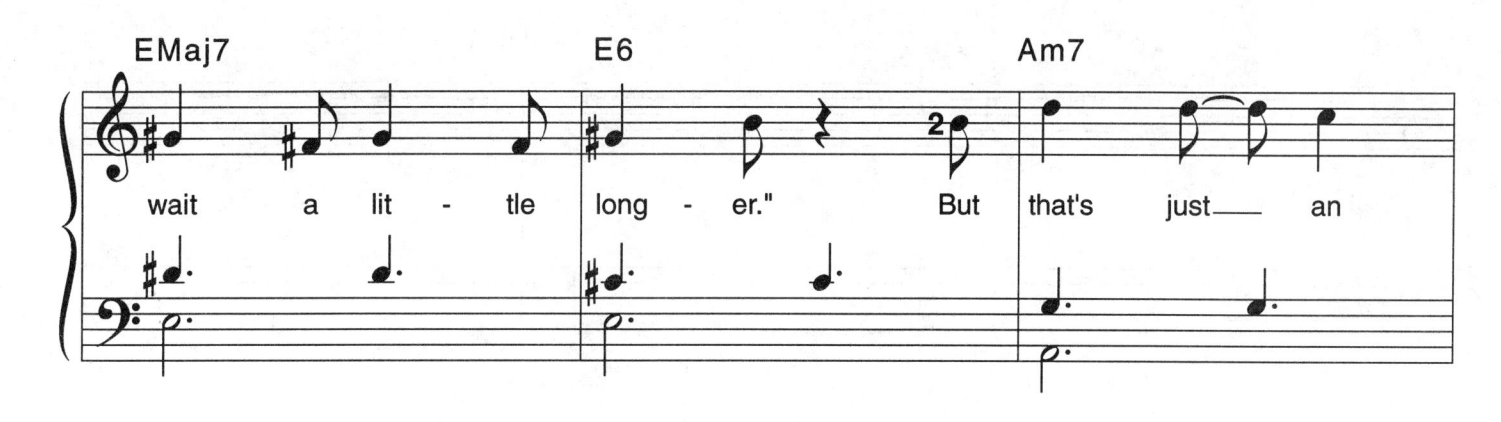

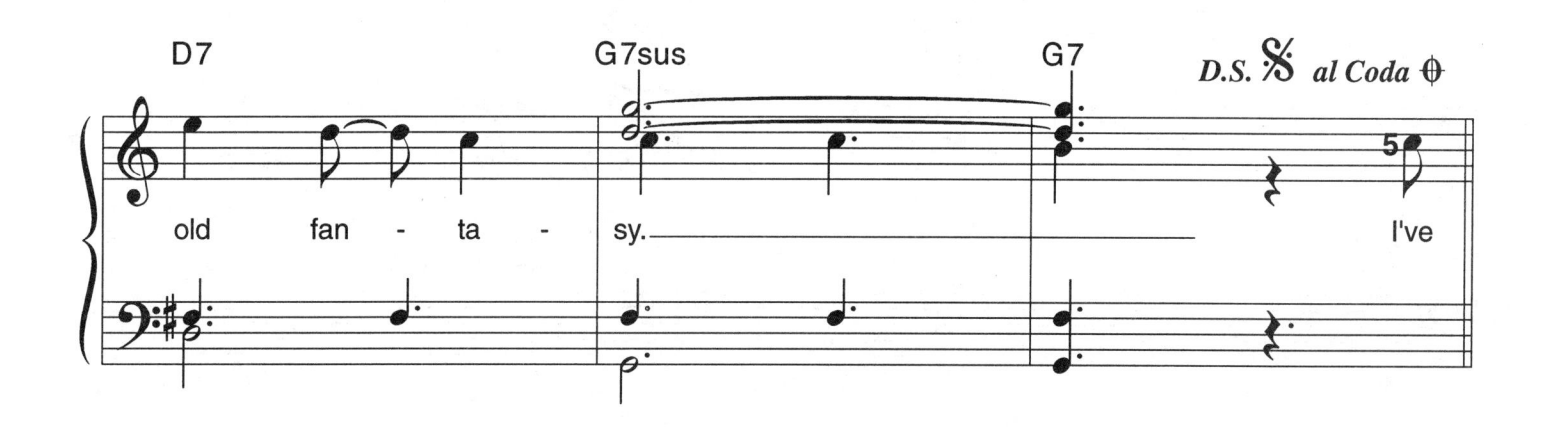

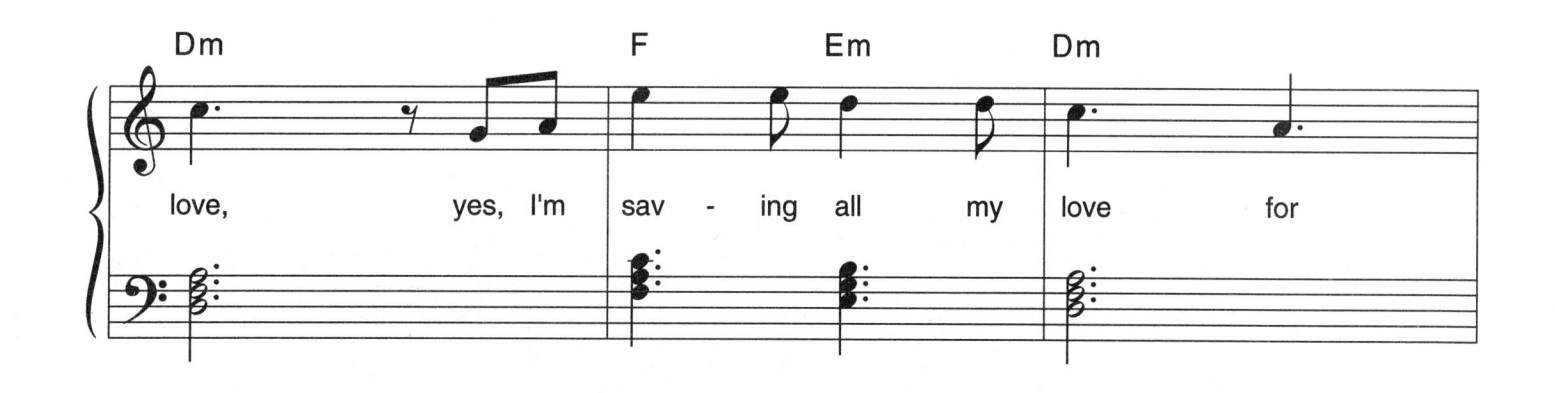

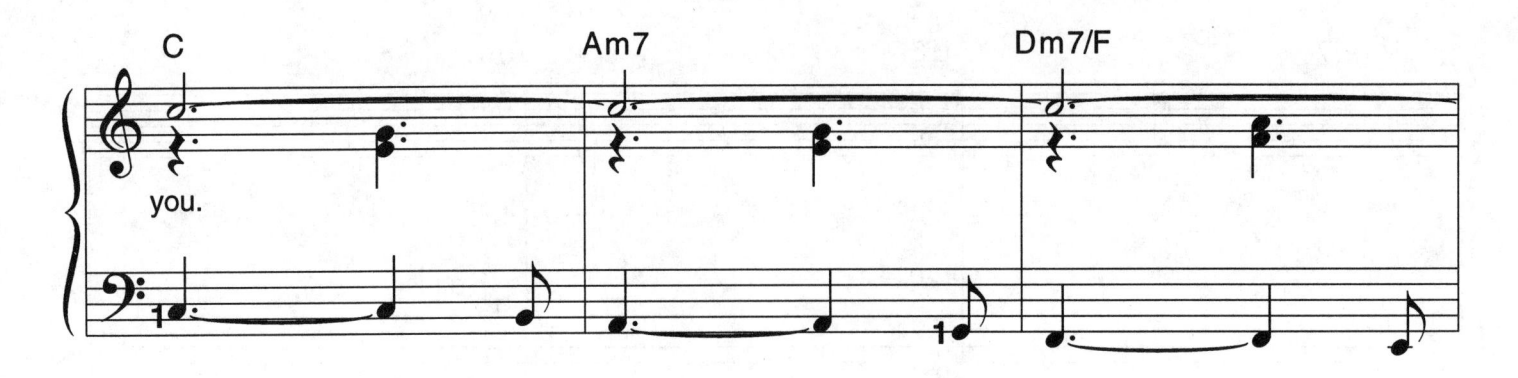

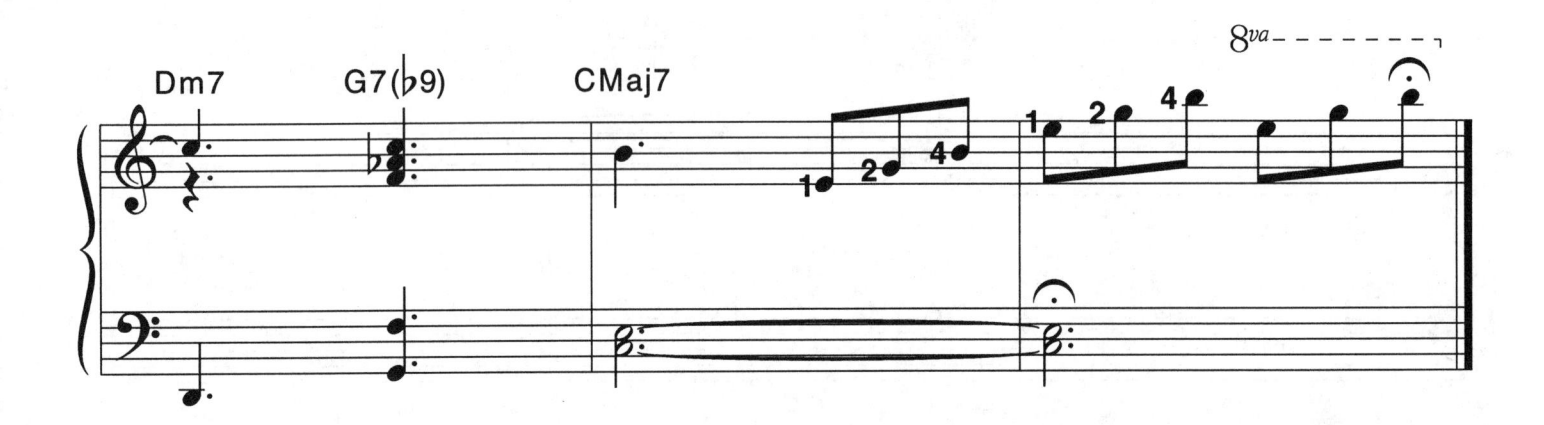

Verse 2:
It's not very easy living all alone.
My friends try and tell me
Find a man of my own.
But each time I try,
I just break down and cry.
'Cause I'd rather be home feelin' blue

From the Motion Picture "ROBIN HOOD: PRINCE OF THIEVES"

(Everything I Do)
I Do It For You

Written by
BRYAN ADAMS, ROBERT JOHN LANGE
and MICHAEL KAMEN
Arranged by Richard Bradley

Look in-to my eyes, you will see
Look in-to your heart, you will find there's

what you mean to me.
noth - ing there to hide.

Search your
So take me

(Everything I Do) I Do It For You - 5 - 1

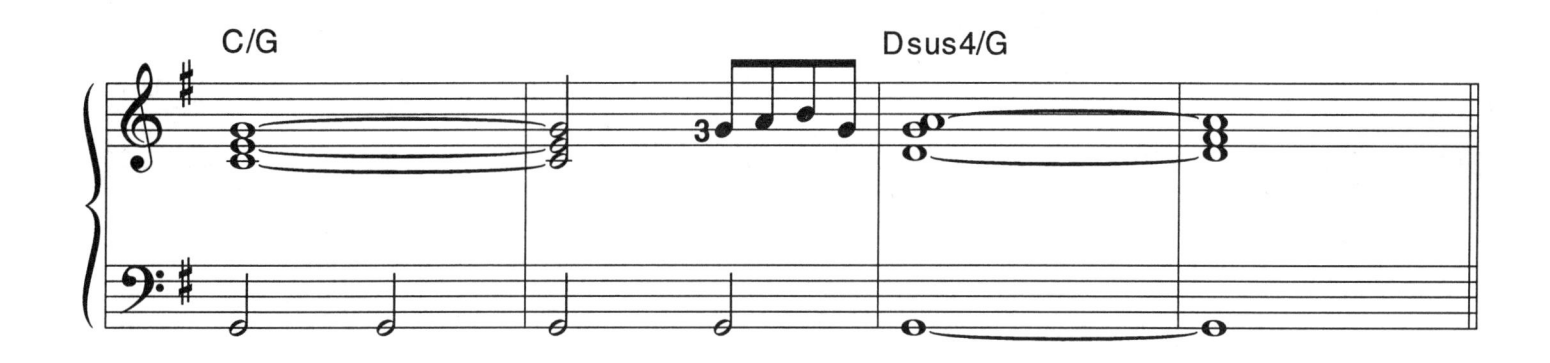

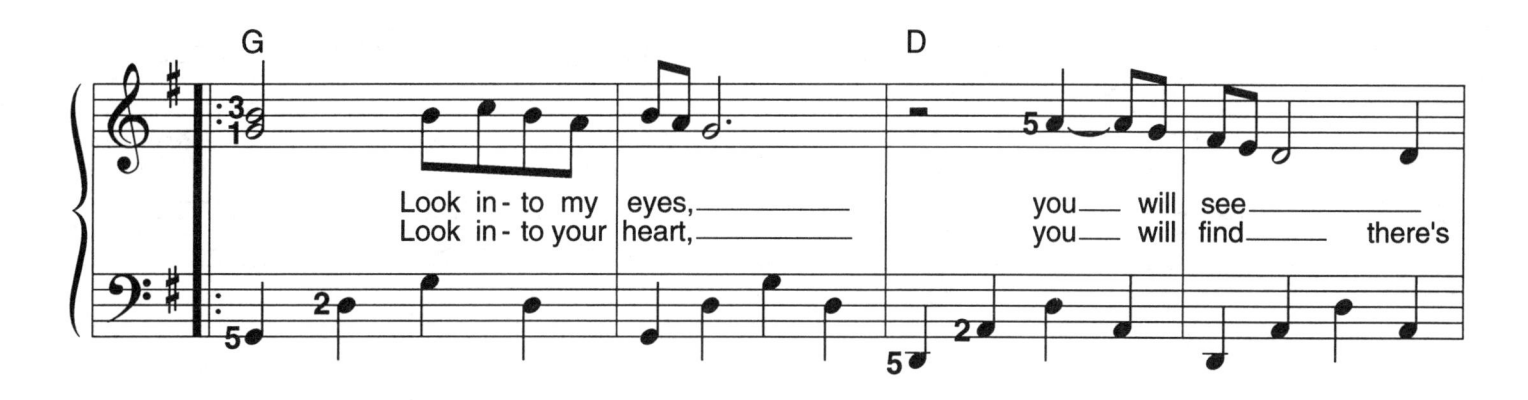

Copyright © 1991 ALMO MUSIC CORP. & ZOMBA PUBLISHING (ASCAP) & ZACHARY CREEK MUSIC, INC. (BMI)
International Copyright Secured   Made in U.S.A.   All Rights Reserved

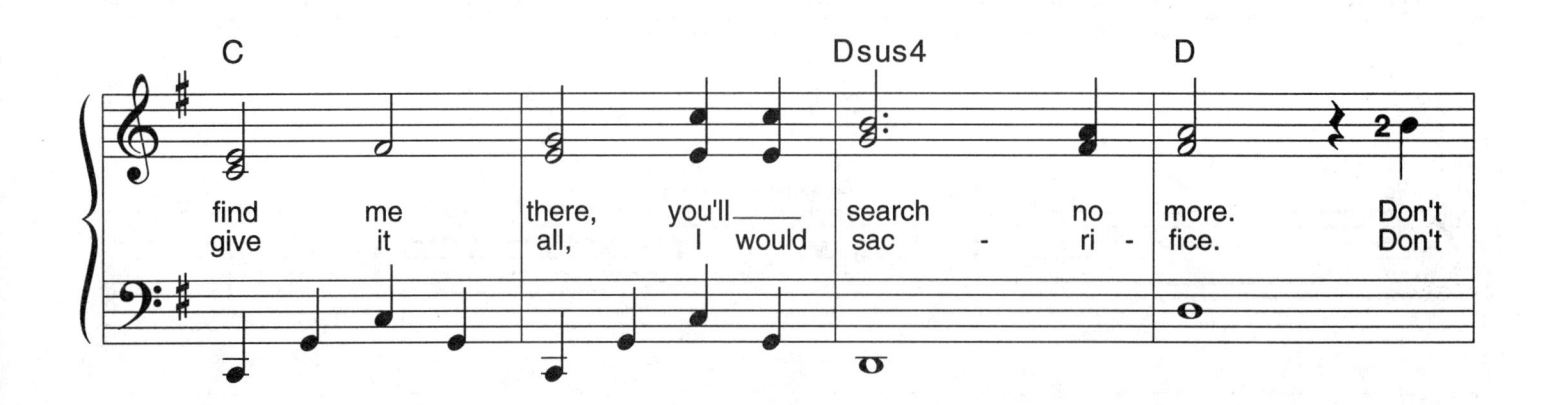

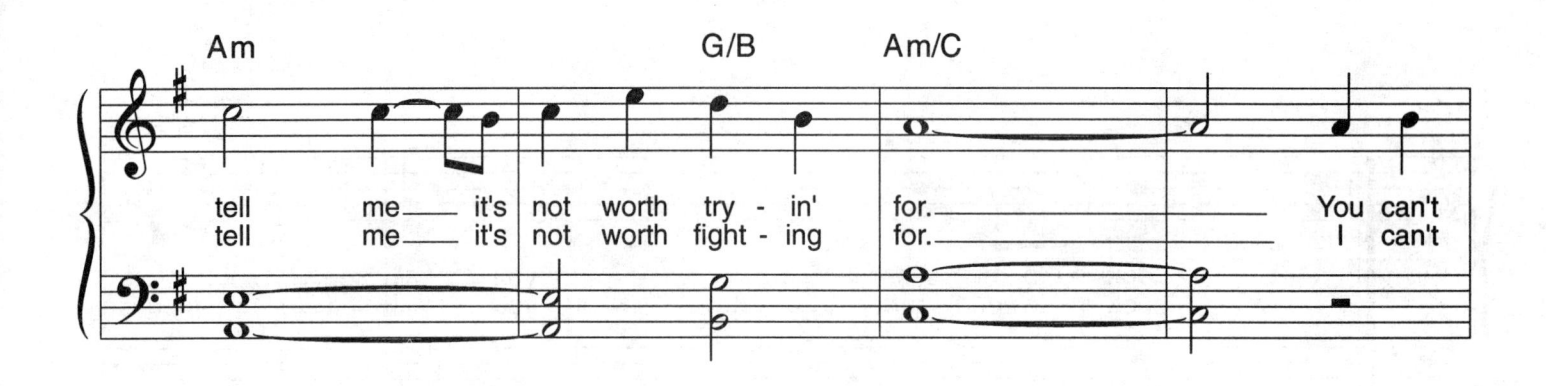

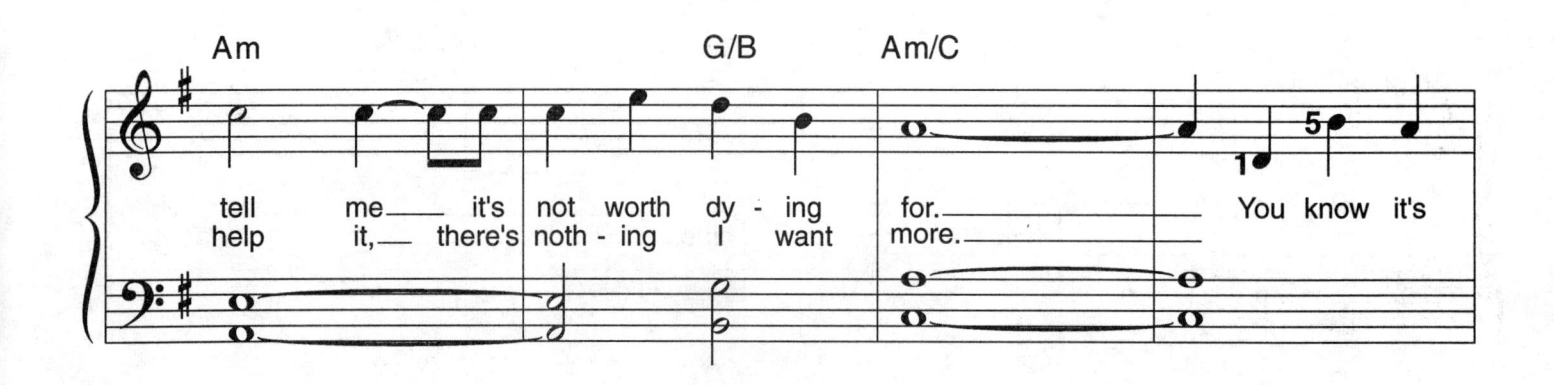

(Everything I Do) I Do It For You - 5 - 2

G
Dsus4
D
true, ev - 'ry - thing I do, I do it for
1.
G
2.
G
you. you. There's
F
B♭
no love like your love, and no
F
C
oth - er could give more love. There's

G
D
no - where un - less you're there, all the
A7
D7
time, all the way. You can't
Am
G/B
Am/C
tell me it's not worth try - in' for. I can't
Am
G/B
Am/C
D7
help it, there's noth - ing I want more. Yeah, I would

G
D
fight for you, I'd lie for you, walk the
C
Cm/E♭
wire for you, I'd die for you. You know it's
G
D
true, ev - 'ry- thing I do, oh,
C
G
oh, I do it for you.

From the Enigma Production, Ladd Company/Warner Bros. Release "CHARIOTS OF FIRE"

Chariots Of Fire

Composed by VANGELIS
Arranged by Richard Bradley

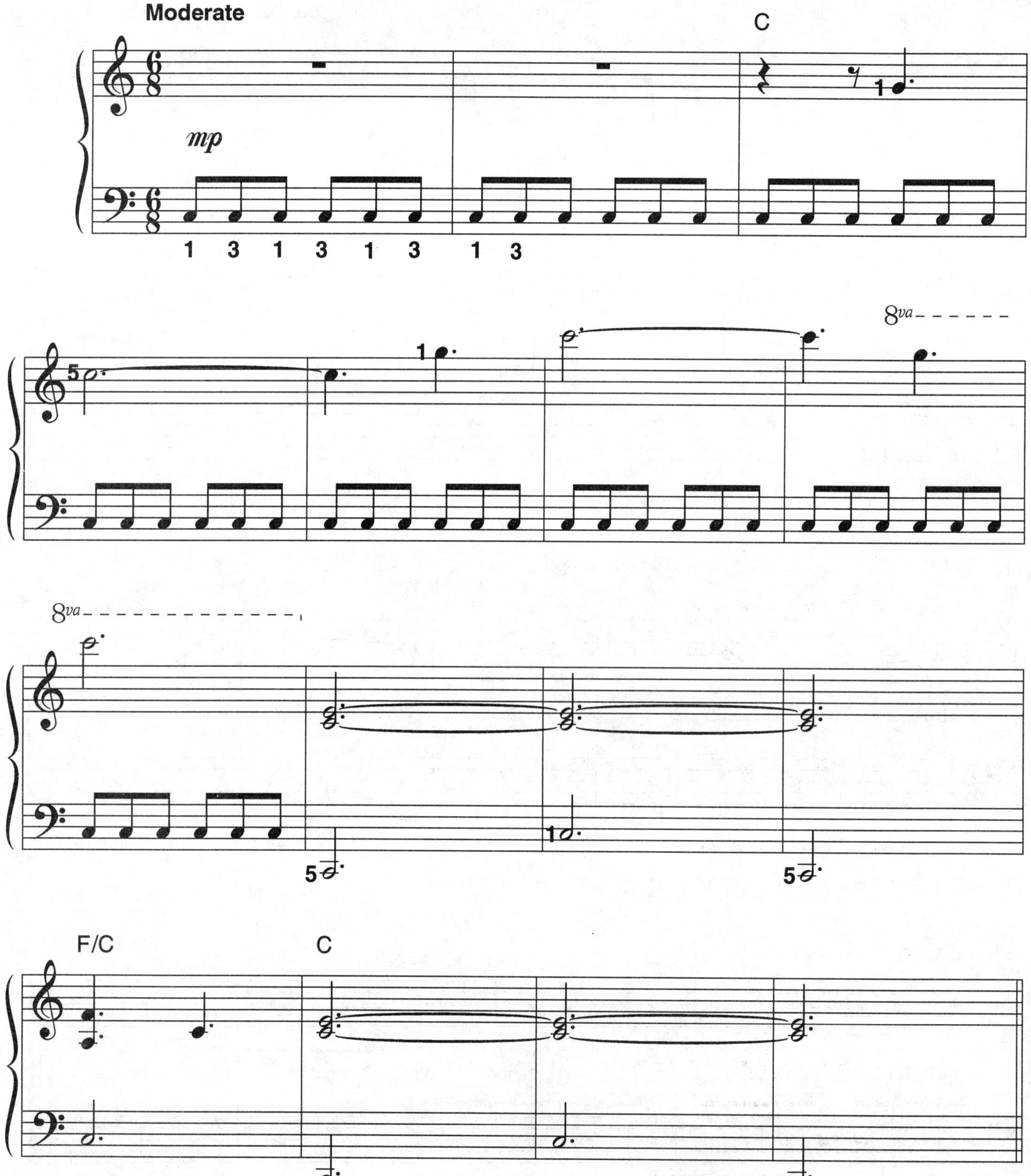

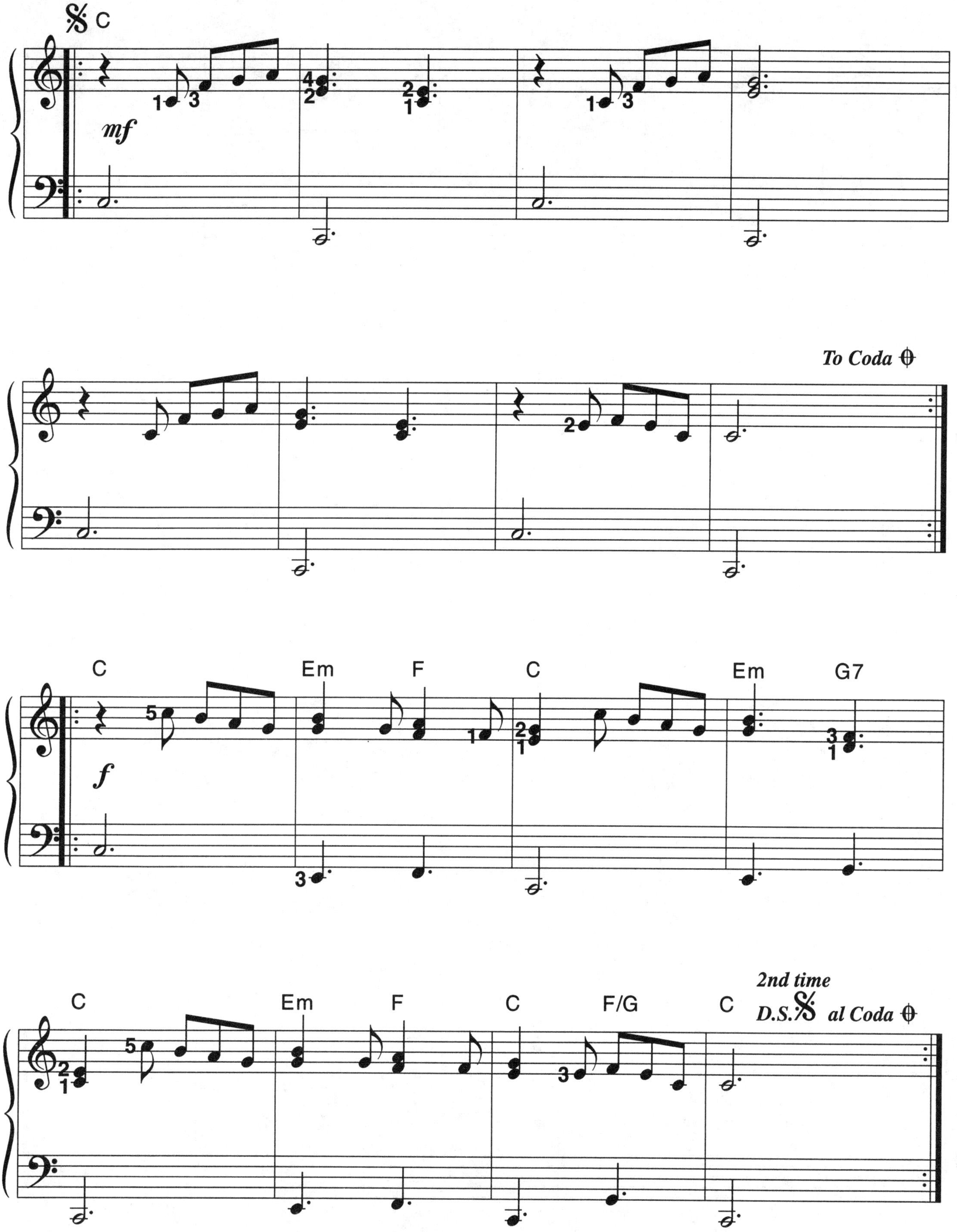
C
mf
To Coda
C
Em
F
C
Em
G7
f
C
Em
F
C
F/G
C
2nd time
D.S. al Coda

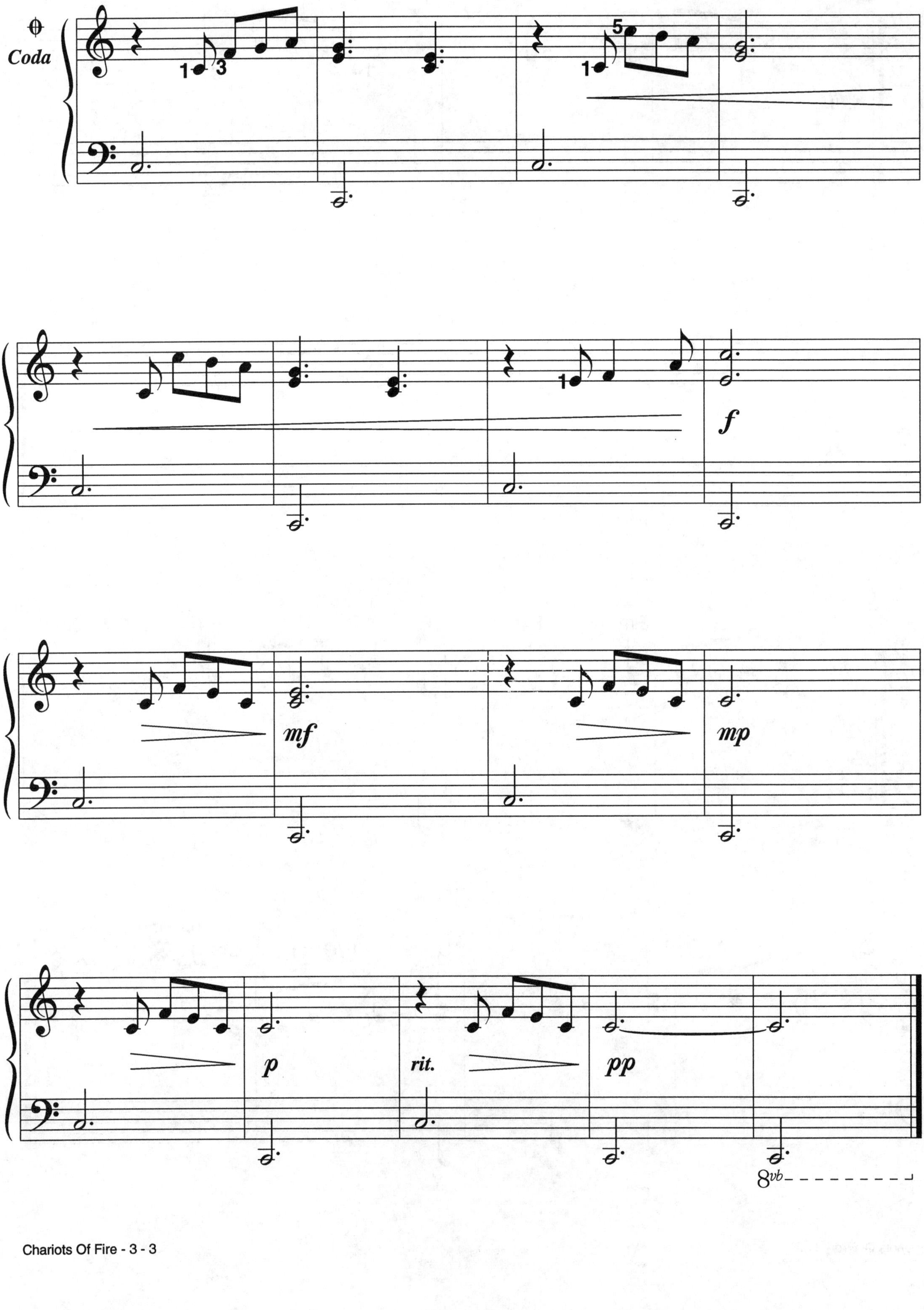
Coda
f
mf
mp
p
rit.
pp
8vb

The Summer Knows
(Theme From "SUMMER OF '42")

Words by
MARILYN and
ALAN BERGMAN

Music by
MICHEL LEGRAND
Arranged by Richard Bradley

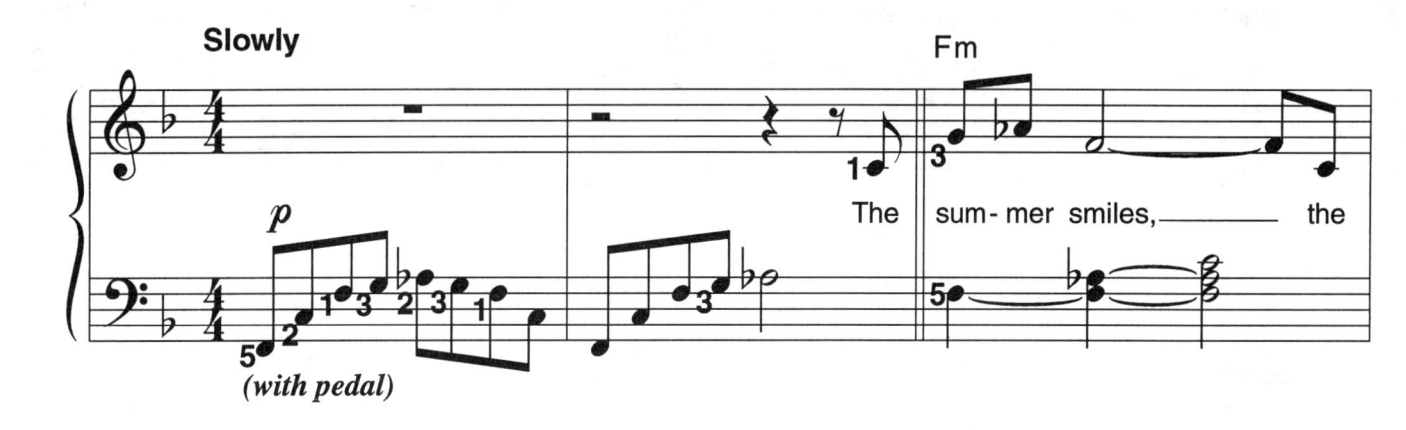

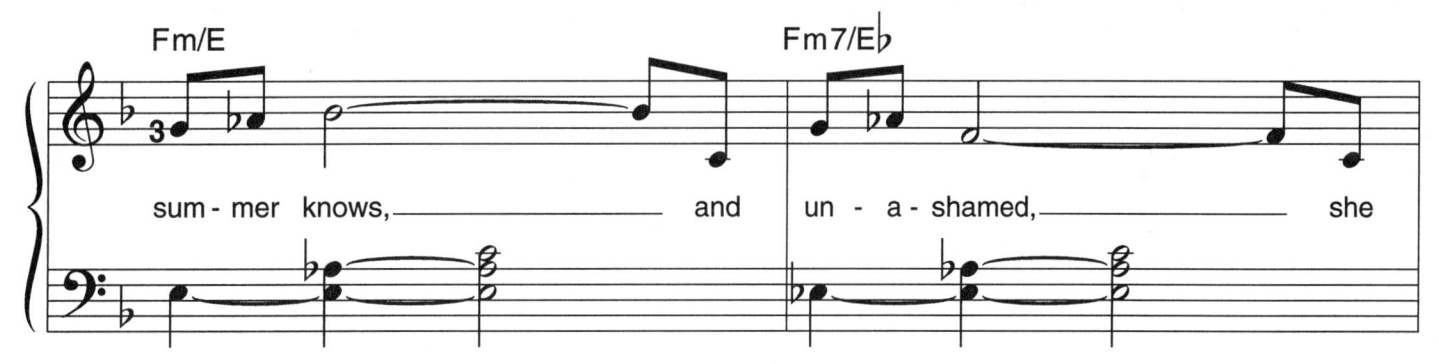

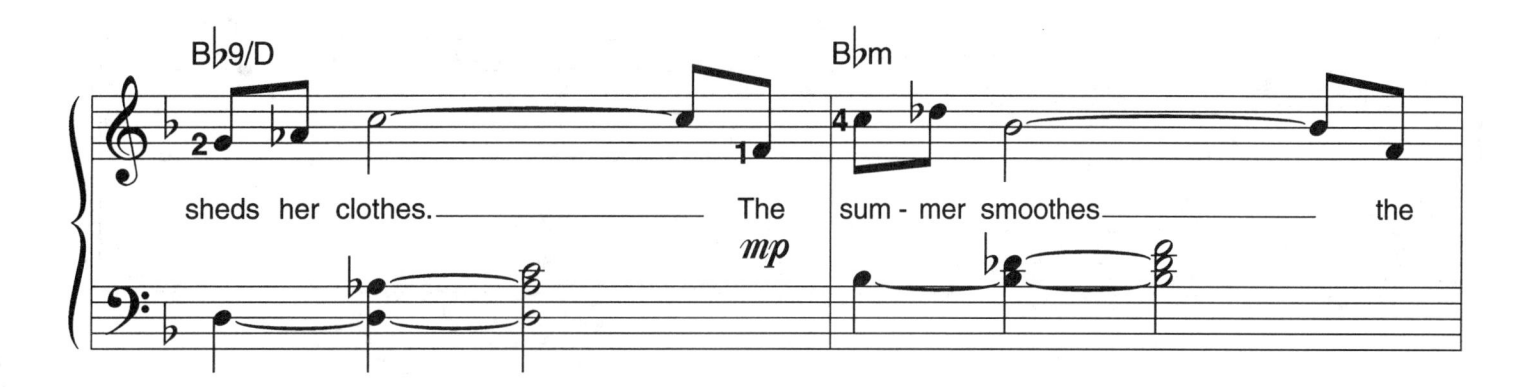

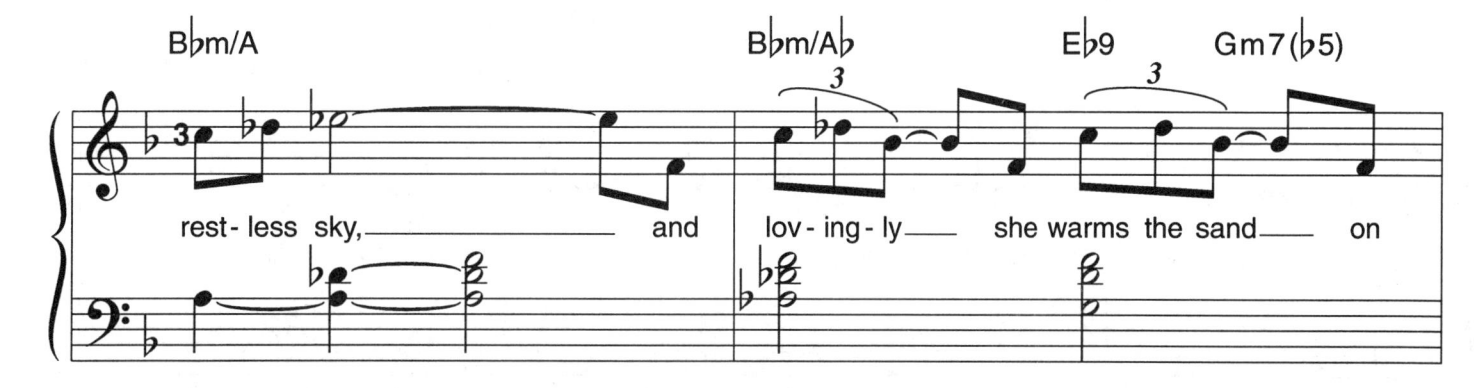

Slowly

The sum-mer smiles, the sum-mer knows, and un-a-shamed, she sheds her clothes. The sum-mer smoothes the rest-less sky, and lov-ing-ly she warms the sand on

The Summer Knows - 3 - 1

© 1971 WB MUSIC CORP.
All Rights Reserved

C7
3
which you lie.
R.H.
The
F2
mf
sum - mer knows,
F
the
B♭m6/F
sum - mer's wise,
B♭m
She
F2
sees the doubts
F
with -
Cm7/F
in your eyes.
F7(♭9)
And
B♭Maj7
so she takes
B♭6
her
B♭
Bm7(♭5)E7
sum mer time,
tells the
AMaj7
moon to
E7
wait and the
AMaj7
sun to
E♭7
lin - ger,

A♭Maj7 E♭7 A♭Maj7 D7 G G+ G6
twists the world 'round her sum - mer fin - ger. Lets you see the
Gm7(♭5) C7(♭9) F2 F B♭m6/F B♭m
won der of it all. And if you've learned your les - son well, there's
mp
F2 F B♭m6/F B♭m Fm
lit - tle more for her to tell, one last ca - ress, it's
p
Gm7(♭5) Fm Fm6add9
time to dress for fall.
molto rit.
pp

The Entertainer

Featured in the Motion Picture "THE STING"

by SCOTT JOPLIN
Arranged by Richard Bradley

F/A
Fm/A♭
C/G
G7/F
C
C7/B♭
F/A
Fm/A♭
C/G
D7/F♯
G7/F
1.C
2. C
To next strain
3. C
8va
Fine
8vb
C
F
Fm
C

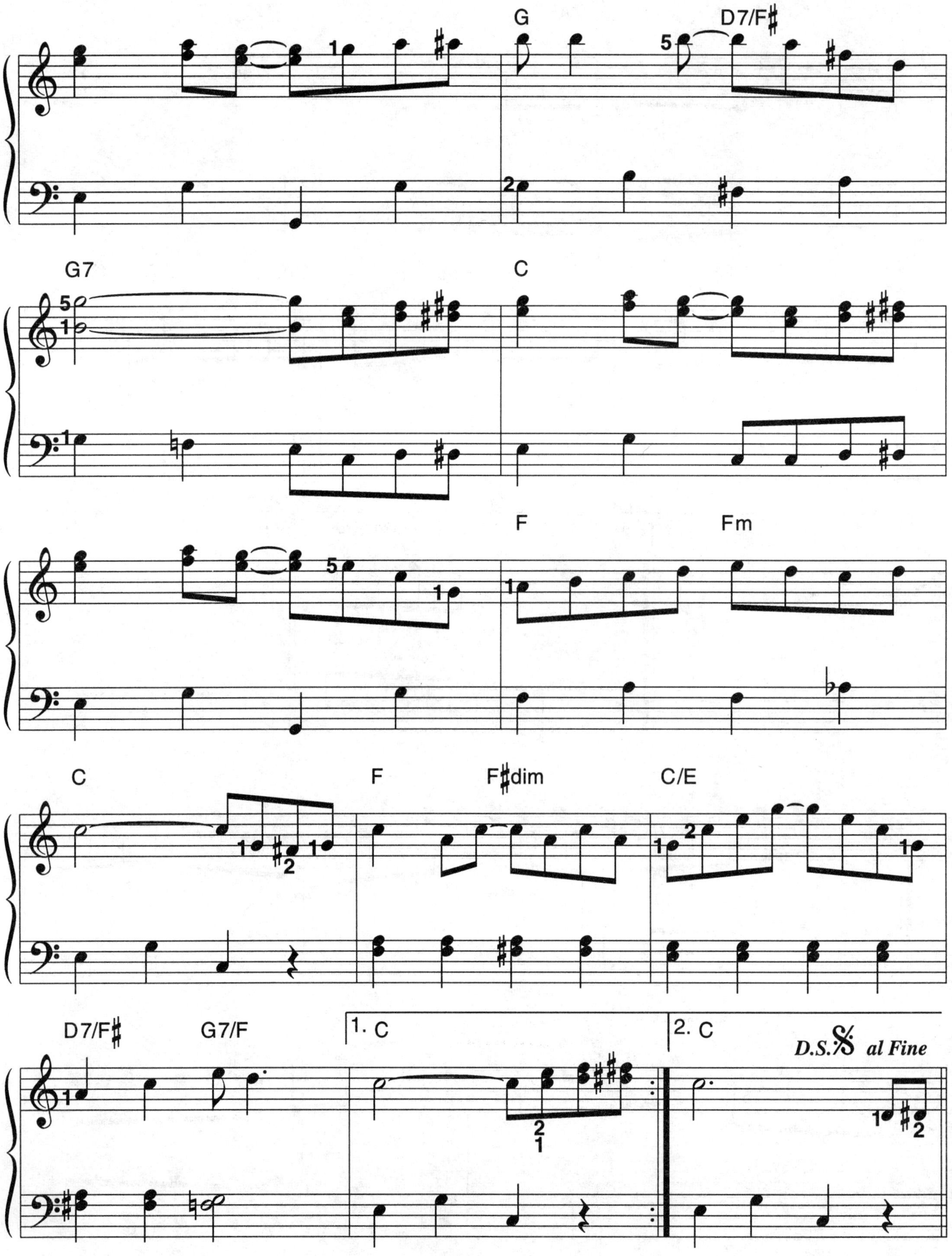
G
D7/F♯
G7
C
F
Fm
C
F
F♯dim
C/E
D7/F♯
G7/F
1. C
2. C
D.S. al Fine

Star Wars
(Main Title)

Music by
JOHN WILLIAMS
Arranged by Richard Bradley

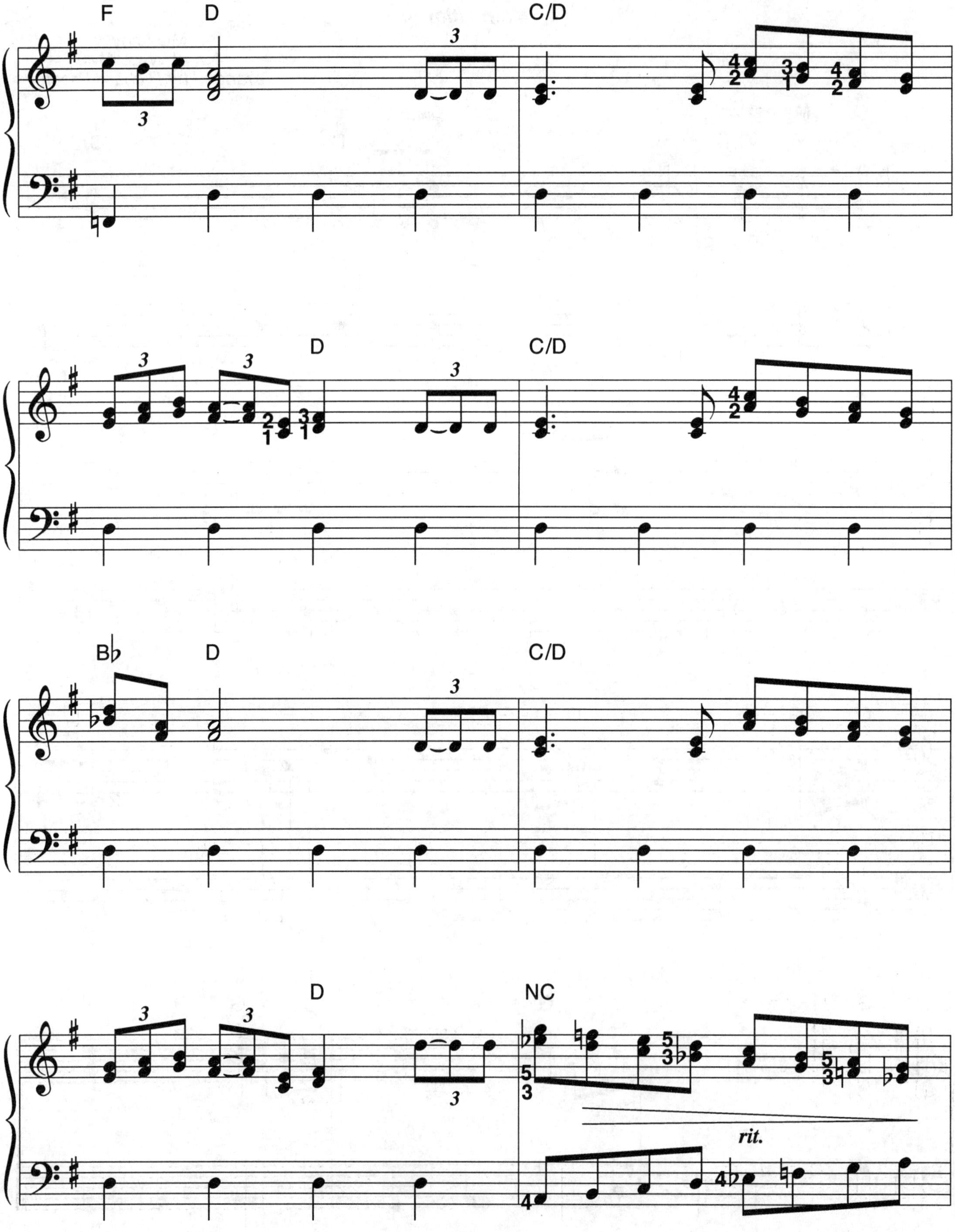
F
D
C/D
D
C/D
B♭
D
C/D
D
NC
rit.

Star Wars - 3 - 3

Oh Happy Day

TRADITIONAL
Arranged by Richard Bradley

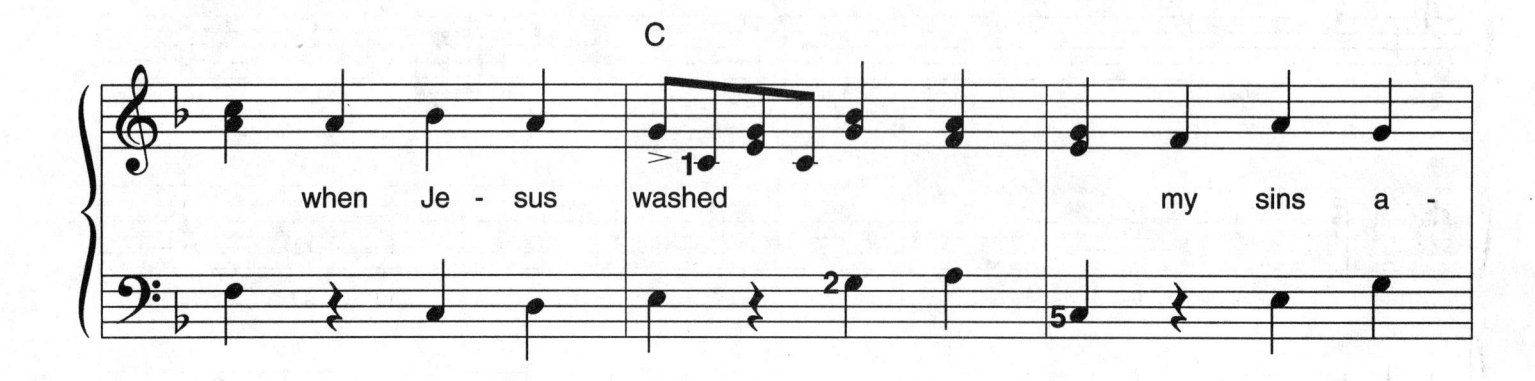

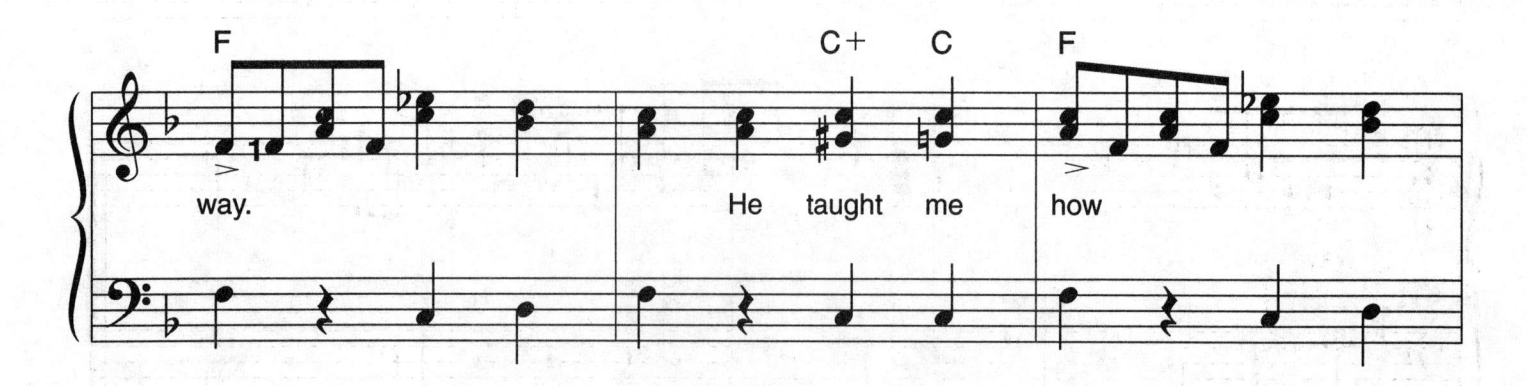

Oh Happy Day - 2 - 2

The Battle Hymn Of The Republic

JULIA WARD HOWE
and WILLIAM STEFFE
Arranged by Richard Bradley

Moderate march tempo

Mine eyes have seen the glory of the coming of the Lord; He is trampling out the vintage where the grapes of wrath are stored; He hath loosed the fateful lightning of His terrible swift sword; His

The Battle Hymn Of The Republic - 2 - 1

Copyright ©1994 BRADLEY PUBLICATIONS
All Rights Assigned to and Controlled by BEAM ME UP MUSIC (ASCAP), c/o CPP/BELWIN, INC.
15800 N.W. 48th Avenue, Miami, FL 33014
International Copyright Secured   Made in U.S.A.   All Rights Reserved

47

Amazing Grace

JOHN NEWTON and
SAMUEL STANLEY
Arranged by Richard Bradley

G G7 C
once was lost but now am
pre cious did that grace ap -
G Em7 A7 D7
found, was blind, but now I
pear the hour I first be -
1. G C G D7
see. 'Twas
2. G G7 G7+
lieved! When
C E7 Dm7/F G7 C
we've been there ten thou - sand years, Bright

50
Am Am7 D7 Dm9 G7
shin - ing as the sun, We've
C C7 F
no less days to sing God's
C Am D7 G7
praise than when we first be -
C
gun.

Fairest Lord Jesus

ANONYMOUS
Arranged by Richard Bradley

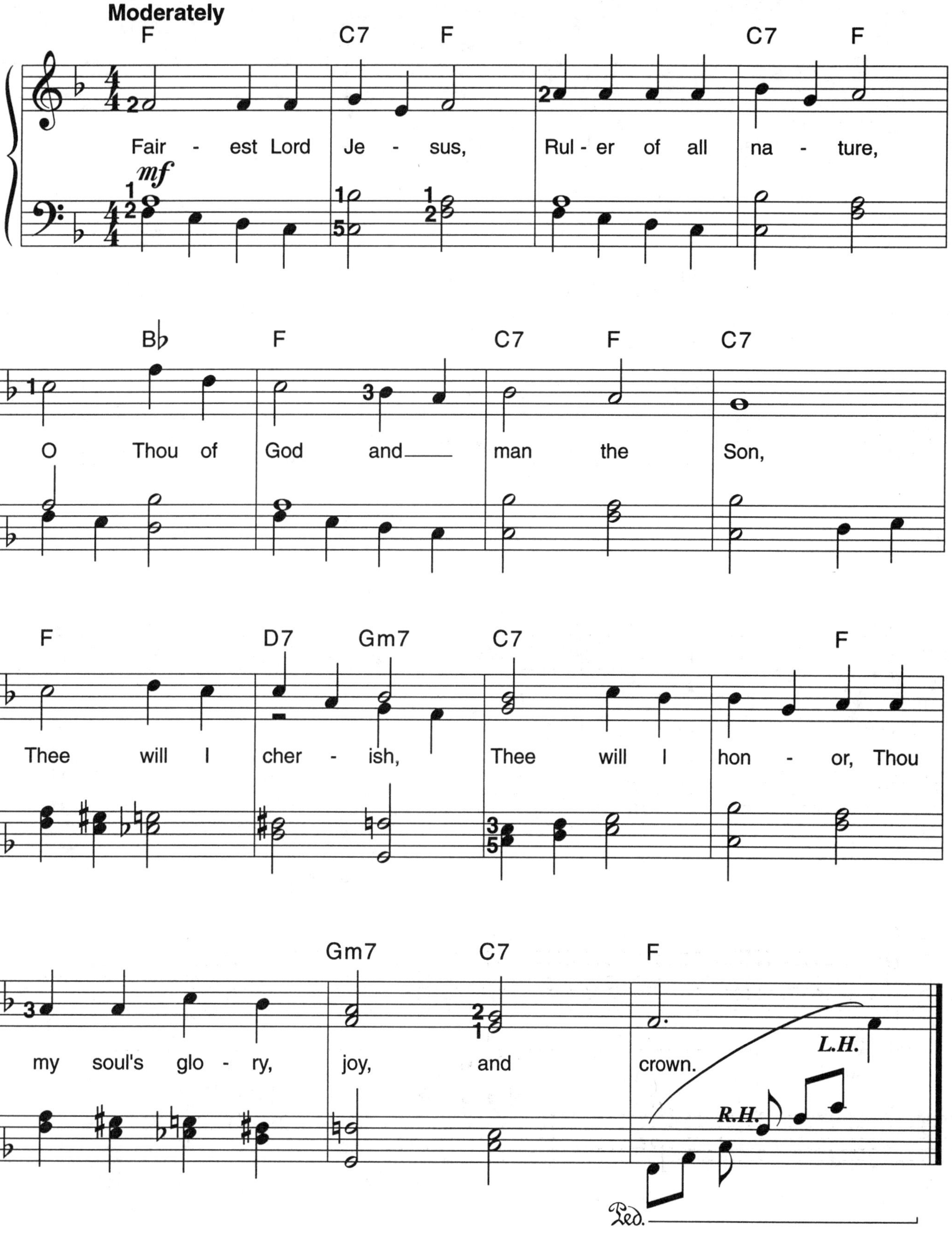

What A Friend We Have In Jesus

JOSEPH SCRIVEN and
CHARLES C. CONVERSE
Arranged by Richard Bradley

Lyrics:
What a friend we have in Je - - sus,
All our sins and grief to bear!
What a priiv - i - lege to car - - ry
Ev - 'ry - thing to God in prayer!

What A Friend We Have In Jesus - 2 - 1

Copyright © 1986, 1994 BRADLEY PUBLICATIONS
All Rights Assigned to and Controlled by BEAM ME UP MUSIC (ASCAP), c/o CPP/BELWIN, INC.
15800 N.W. 48th Avenue, Miami, FL 33014
International Copyright Secured   Made in U.S.A.   All Rights Reserved

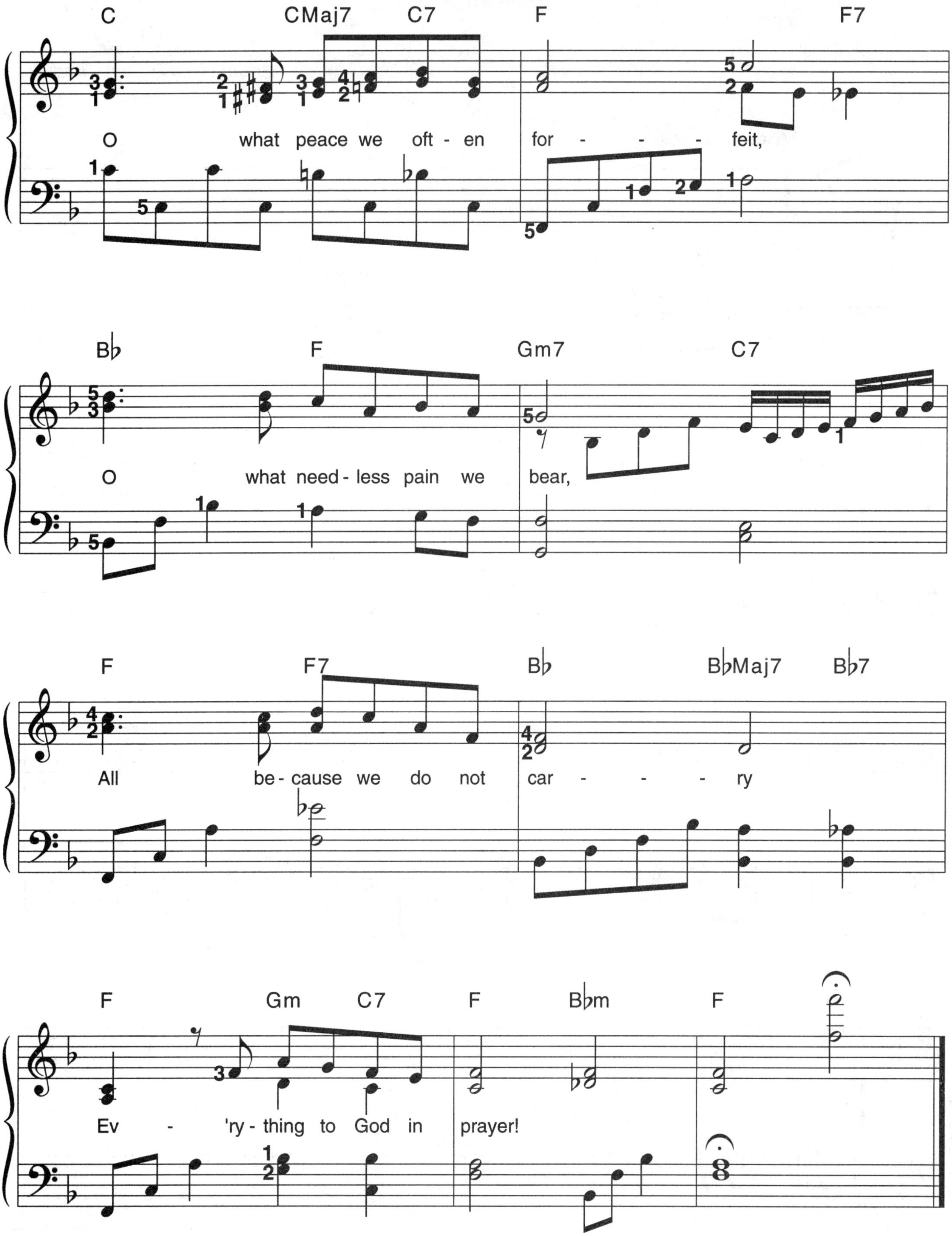
C CMaj7 C7 F F7
O what peace we oft - en for - - - feit,
B♭ F Gm7 C7
O what need - less pain we bear,
F F7 B♭ B♭Maj7 B♭7
All be - cause we do not car - - - ry
F Gm C7 F B♭m F
Ev - 'ry - thing to God in prayer!

Beverly Hills, 90210
(Main Theme)

By
JOHN E. DAVIS
Arranged by Richard Bradley

Beverly Hills, 90210 - 4 - 1

© 1990, 1992 HOT & TANGY MUSIC
All rights administered by WB MUSIC CORP.
All Rights Reserved

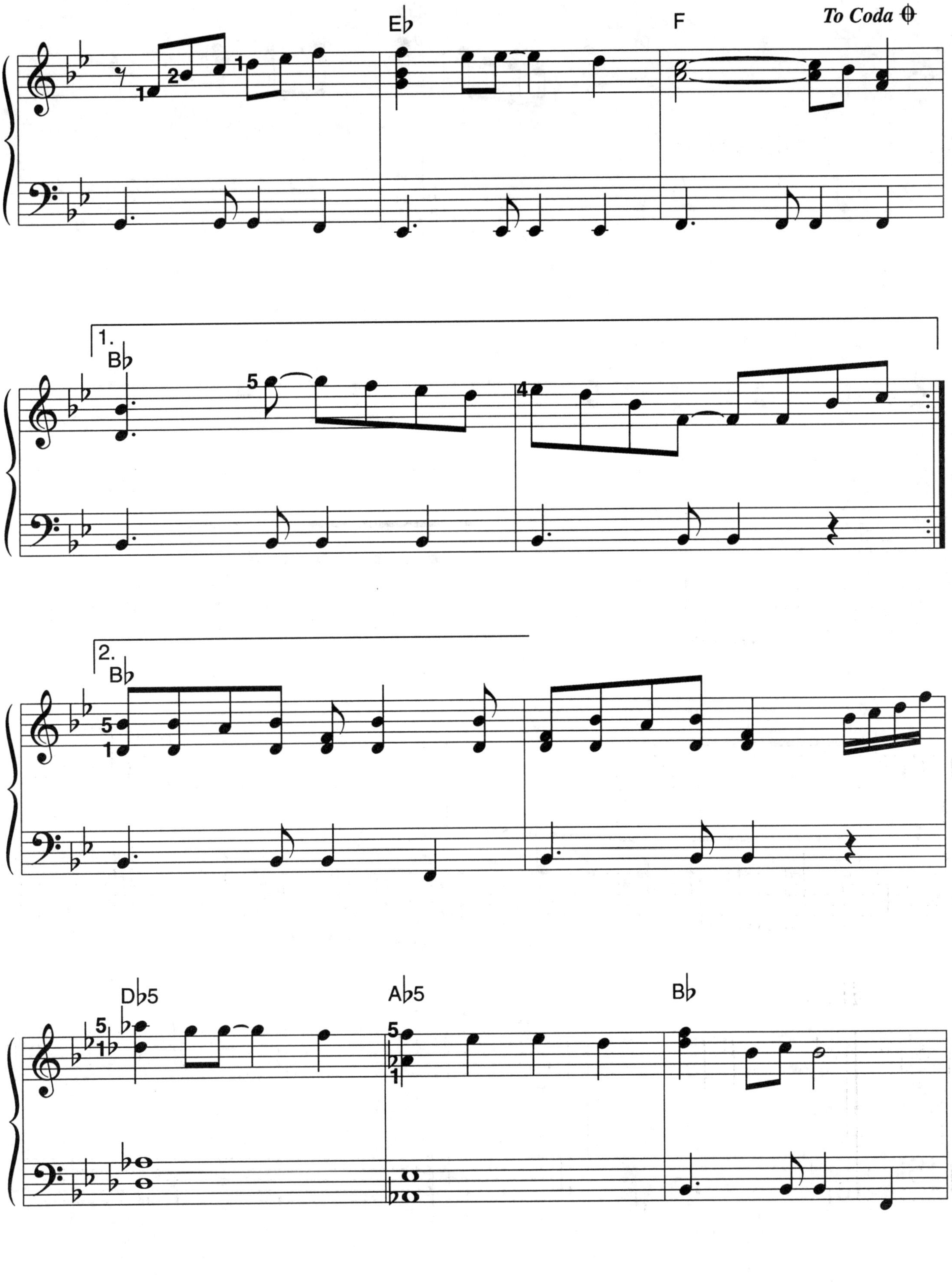
E♭
F
To Coda
1.
B♭
2.
B♭
D♭5
A♭5
B♭

Beverly Hills, 90210 - 4 - 3

Eb5 Bb5 Db5 Ab5
D.S. al Coda
Bb5 Db5 Eb5 F5 Gb5 Ab5
Coda
Bb Gb Ab
Bb Gb5 Ab5 Bb

Ashokan Farewell
From the Soundtrack of PBS Series "THE CIVIL WAR", a film by Ken Burns

By
JAY UNGAR
Arranged by Richard Bradley

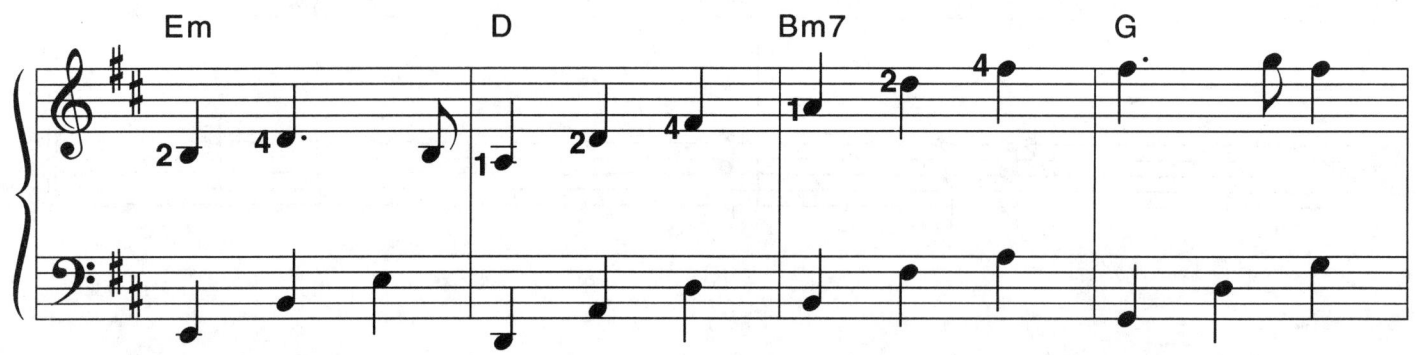

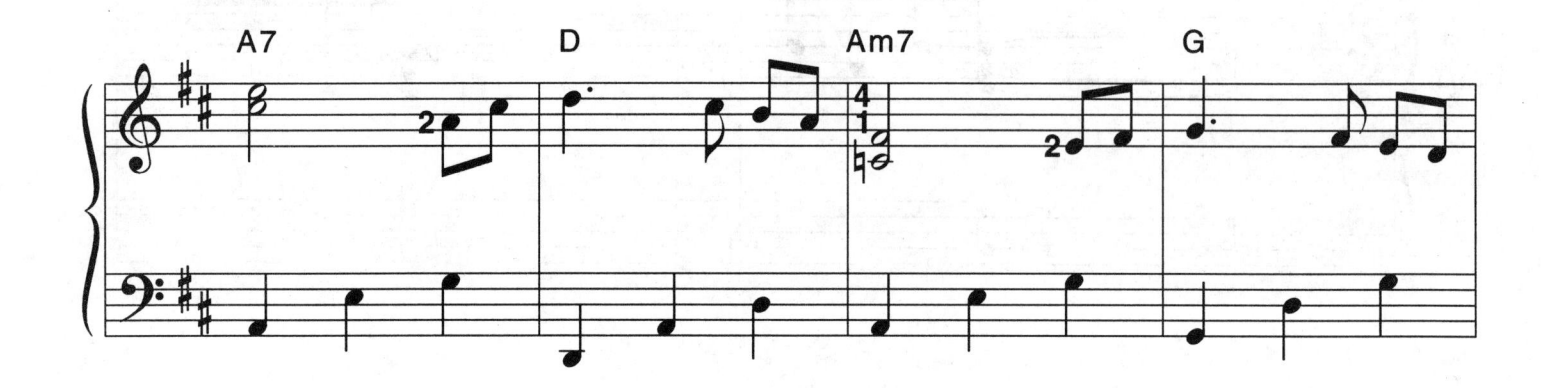

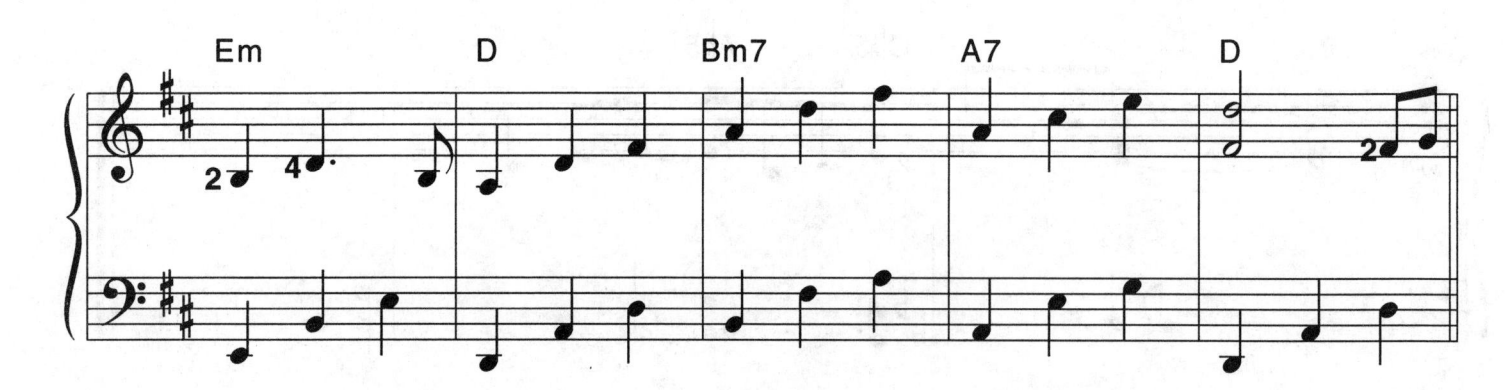

Ashokan Farewell - 2 - 2

Moonlighting

Words by
AL JARREAU

Music by
LEE HOLDRIDGE
Arranged by Richard Bradley

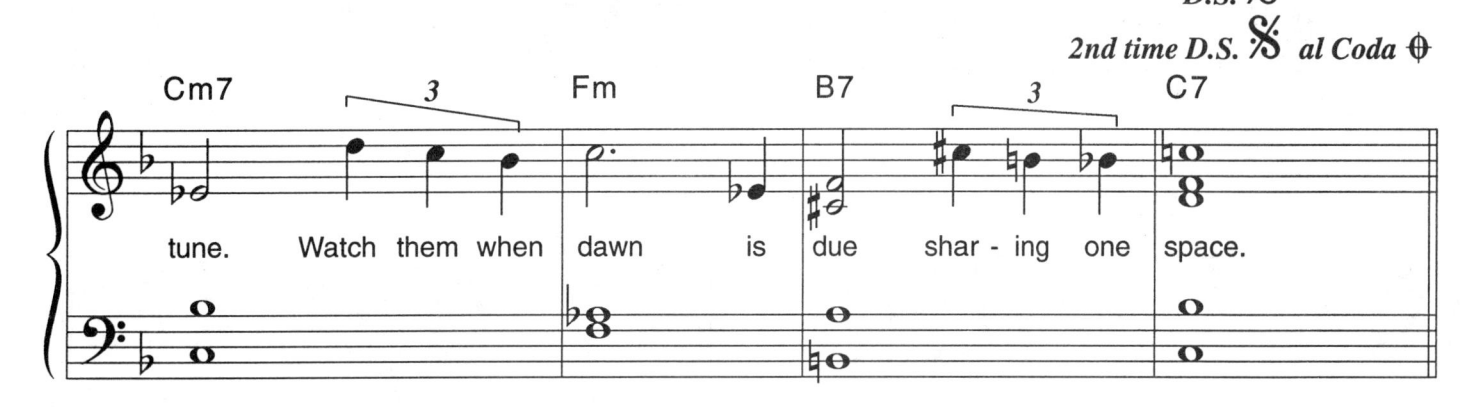

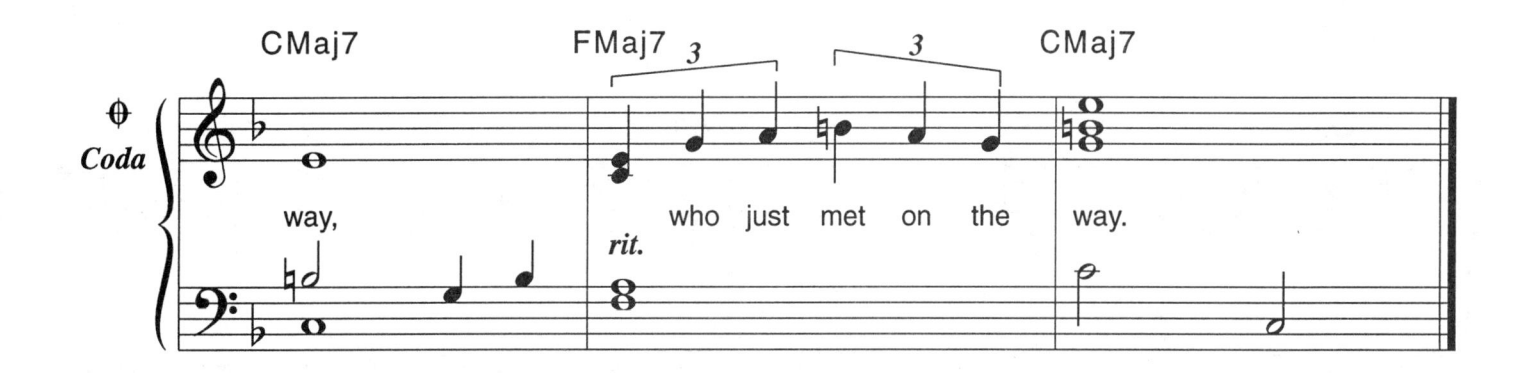

Verse 2:
Charming and bright,
Laughing and gay.
I'm just a stranger,
Love the Blues and the Braves.

Verse 3:
Some walk by night,
Some walk by day.
Something is sweeter
When you meet 'long the way.

Verse 4:
So come walk the night,
Come fly by day.
Something is sweeter
'Cause we met 'long the way.

Verse 5:
We'll walk the night,
We'll fly by day.
Moonlighting strangers
Who just met in the way,
Who just met on the way.

Theme of "ALFRED HITCHCOCK PRESENTS"

Funeral March Of The Marionettes

Composed by
CHARLES GOUNOD
Arranged by Richard Bradley

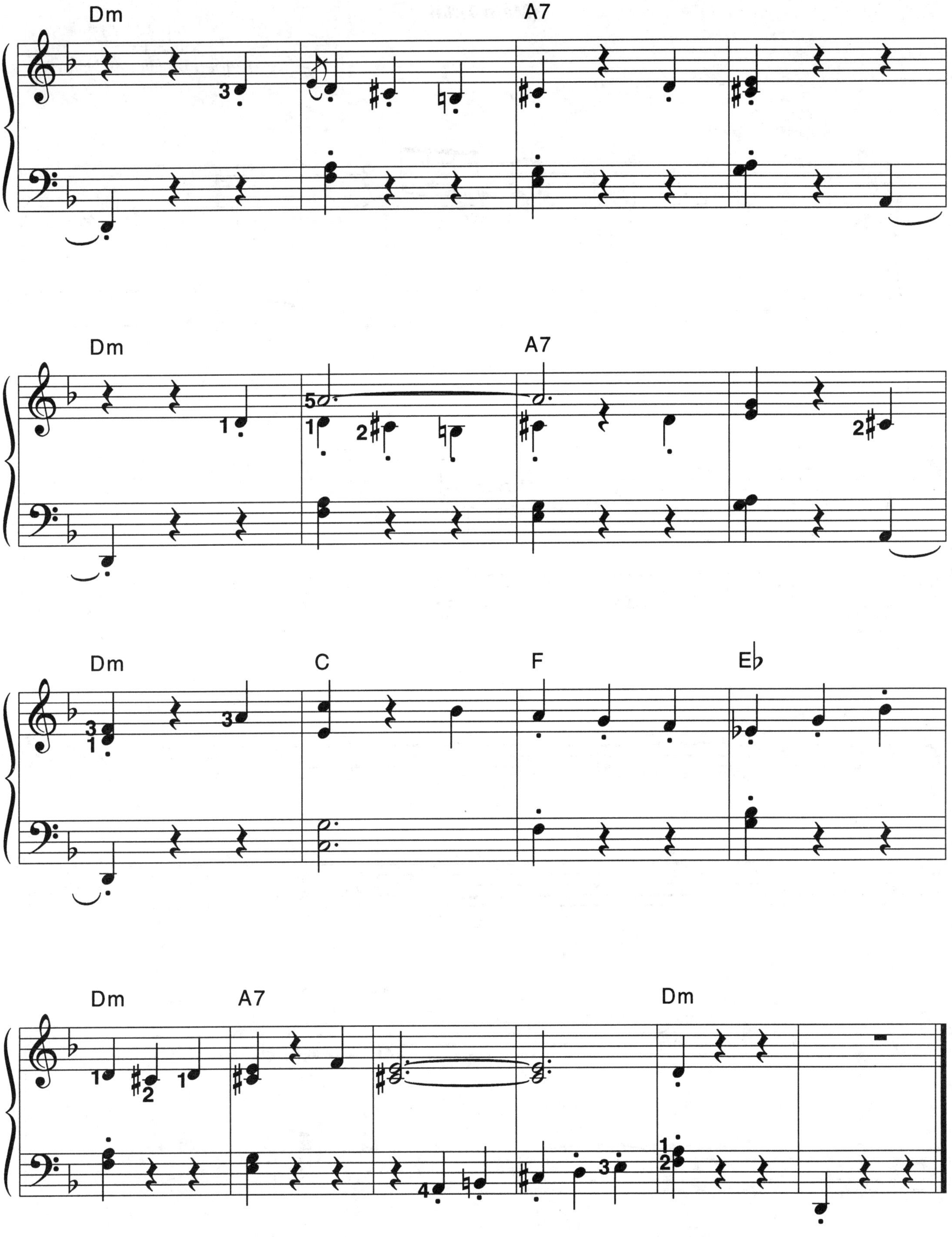
Dm
A7
Dm
A7
Dm
C
F
E♭
Dm
A7
Dm

L.A. Law
(Main Title)

Music by
MIKE POST
Arranged by Richard Bradley

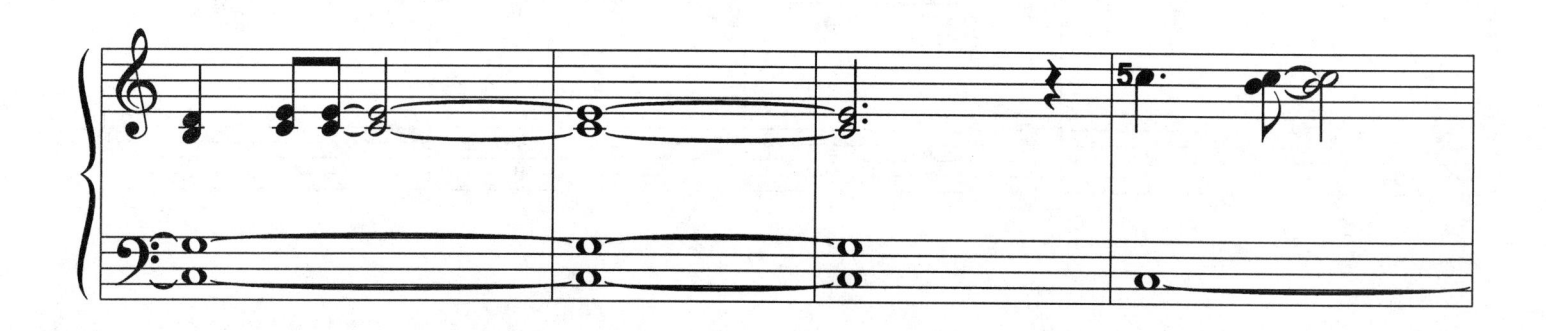

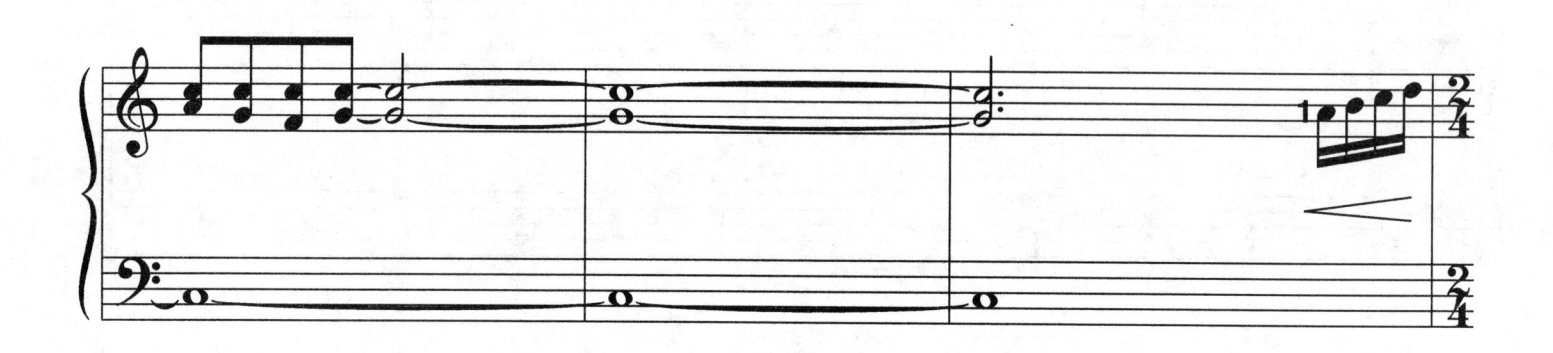

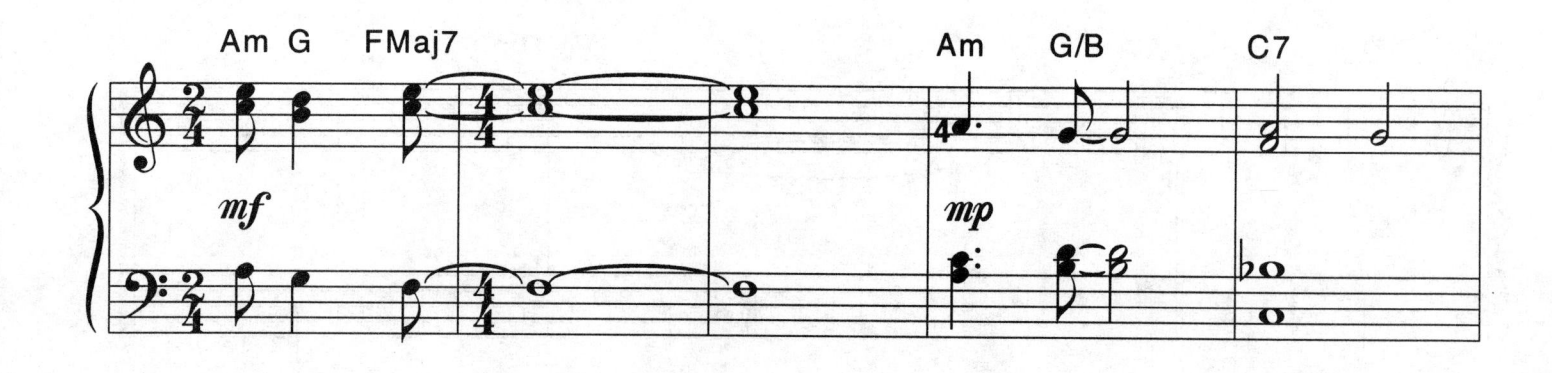

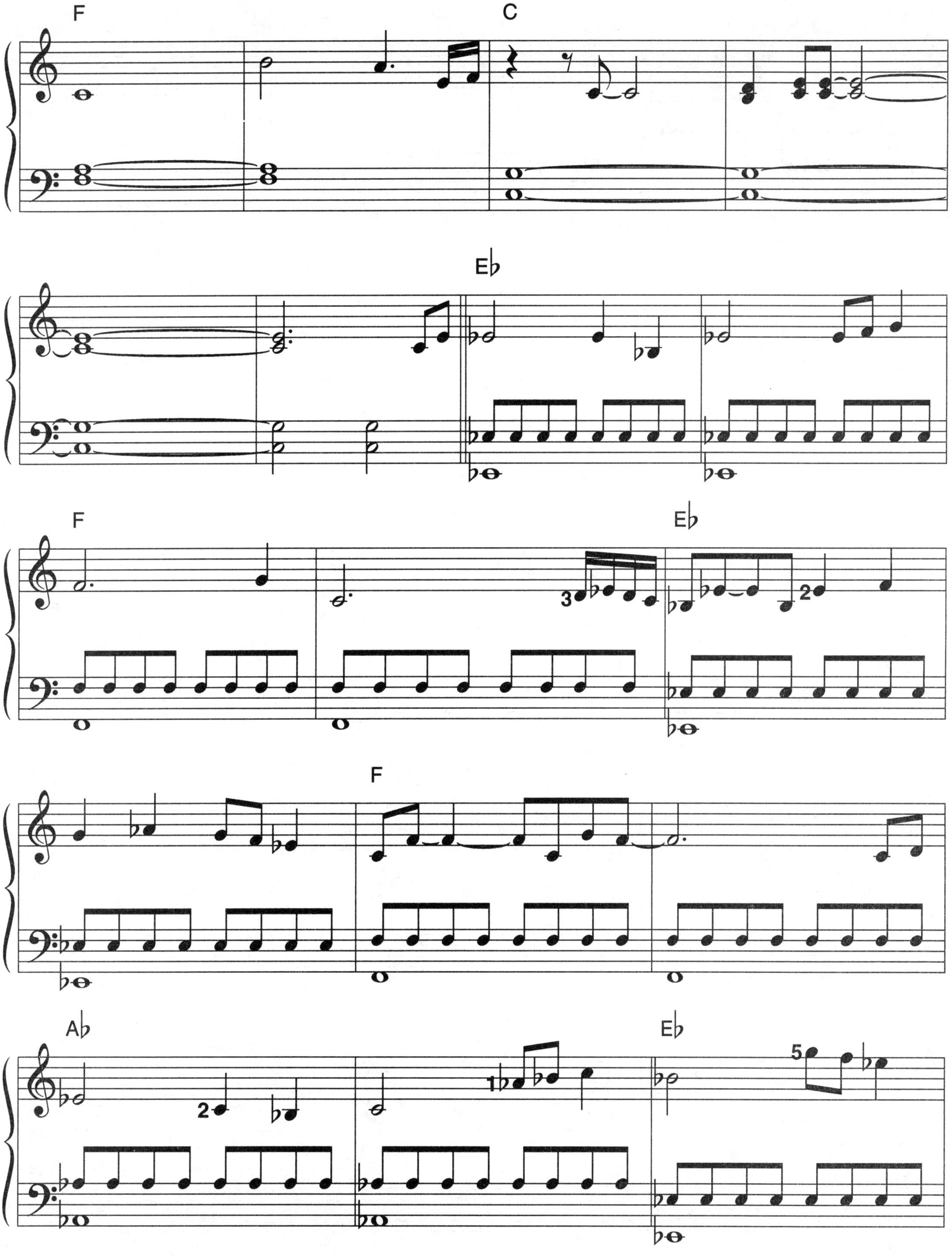
F
C
E♭
F
3
E♭
2
F
A♭
2
1
E♭
5

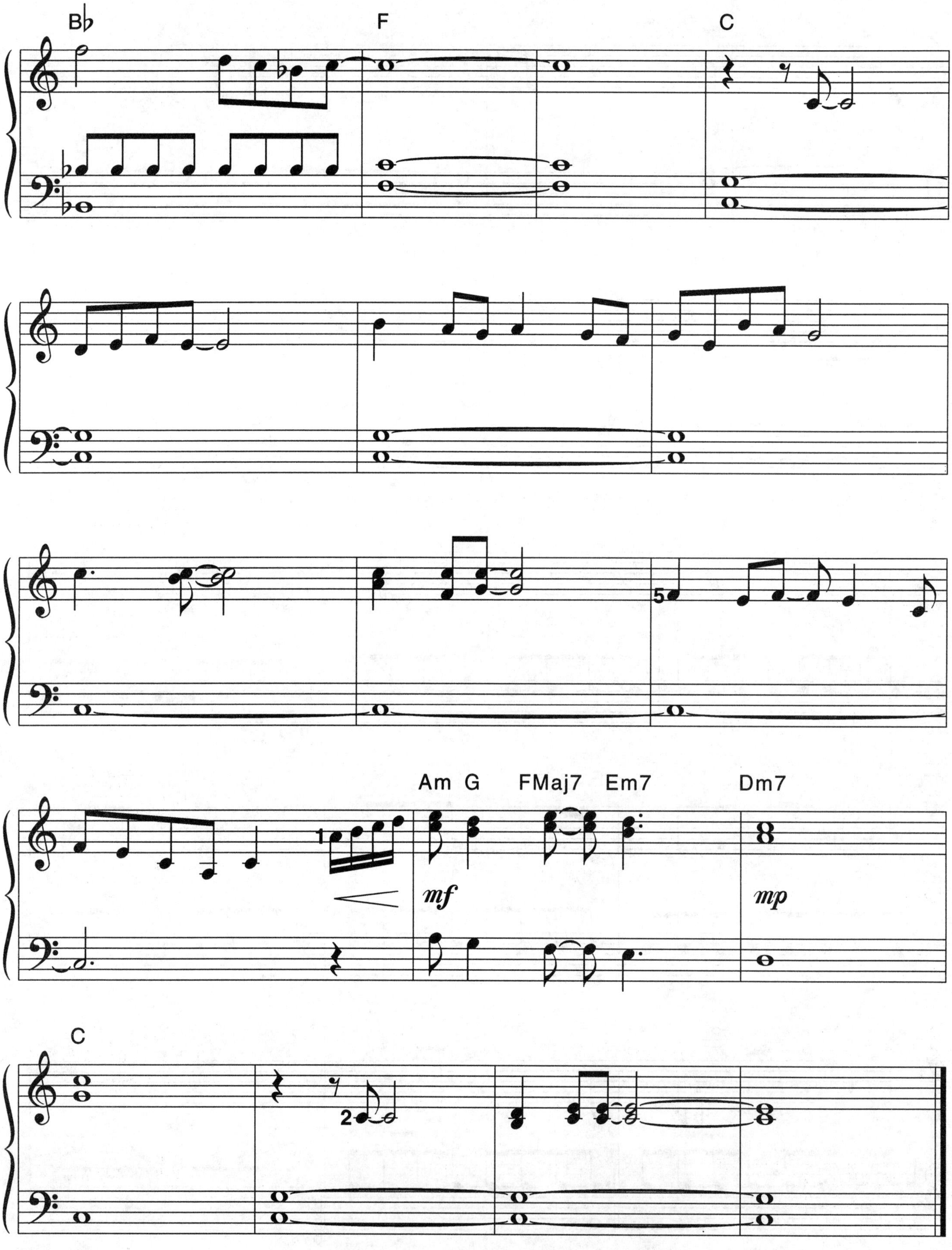
B♭
F
C
Am G
FMaj7
Em7
Dm7
mf
mp
C

Basis For The Music From "FANTASIA"

The Sorcerer's Apprentice

Composed by
PAUL DUKAS
Arranged by Richard Bradley

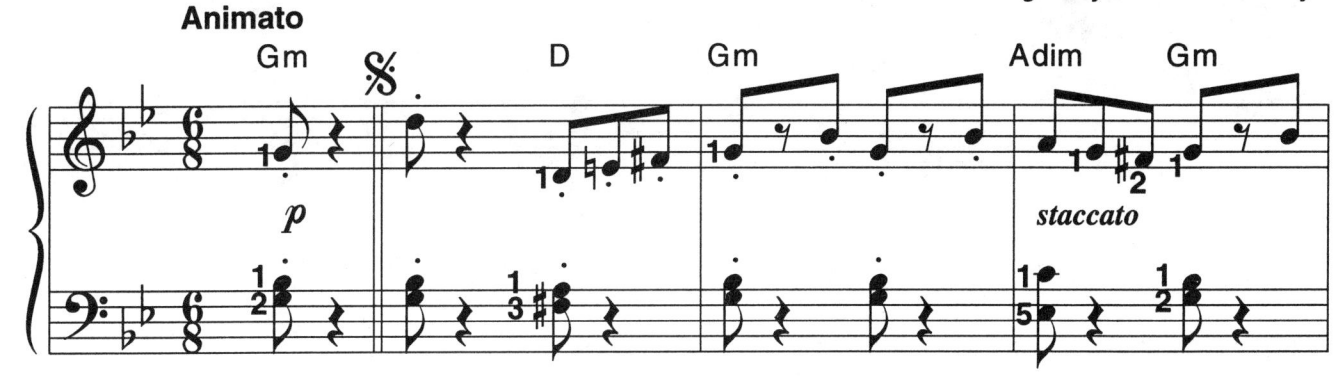

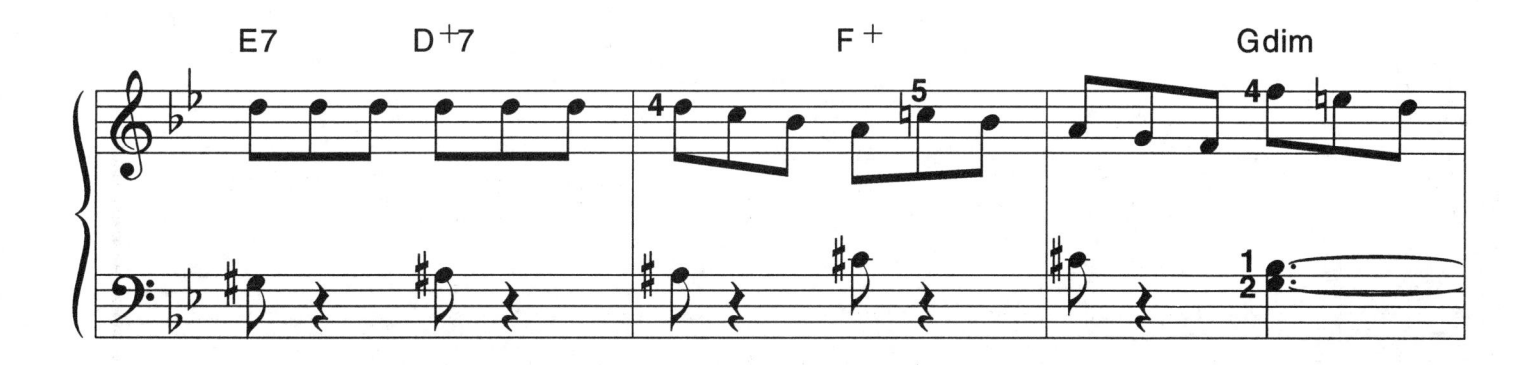

Animato

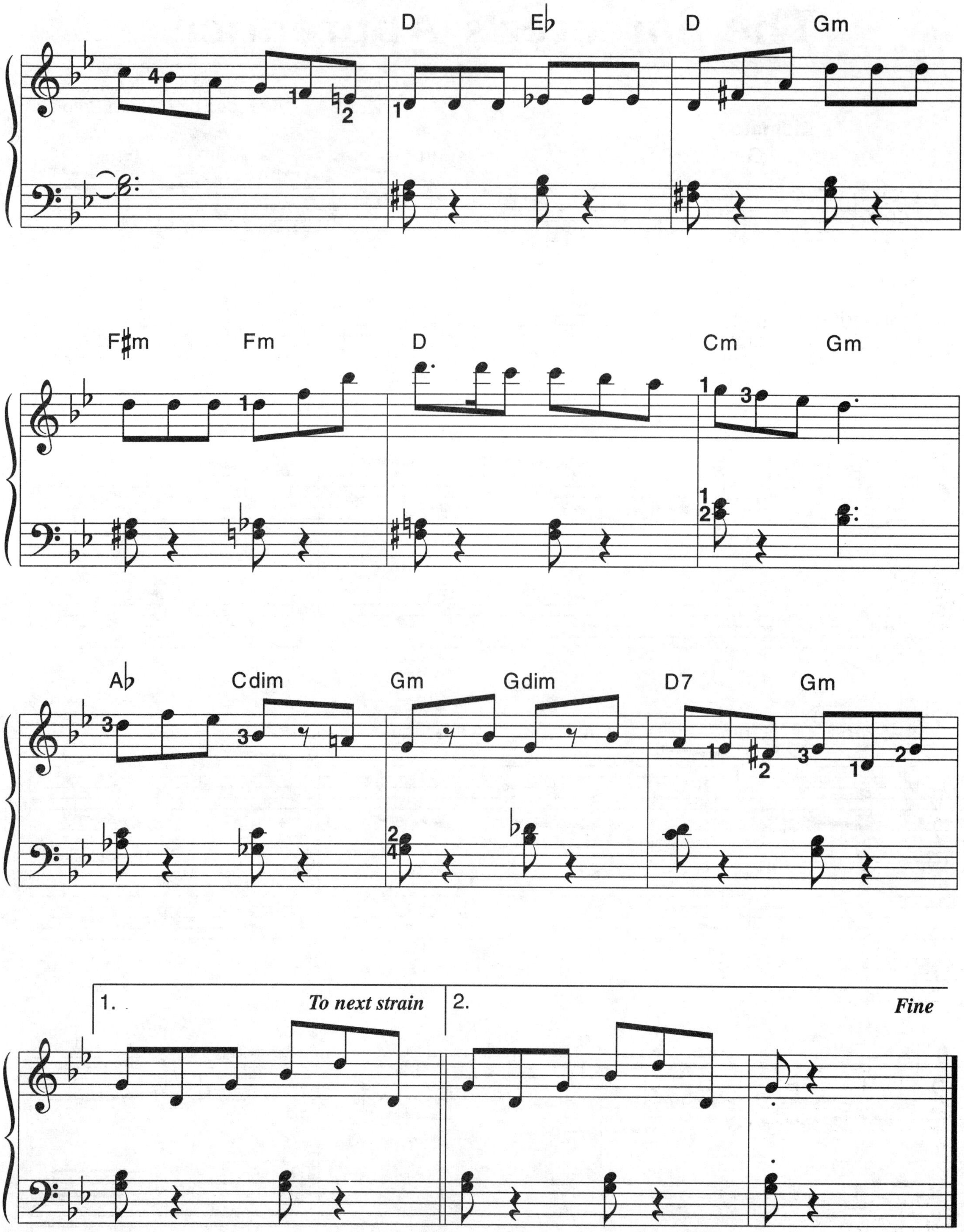
D
E♭
D
Gm
F♯m
Fm
D
Cm
Gm
A♭
Cdim
Gm
Gdim
D7
Gm
1.
To next strain
2.
Fine

E♭
E♭+
E♭6
f legato
mp
staccato
E♭+
E♭6
E♭+
E♭
legato
E♭+
staccato
legato
D7
staccato
Gm
D.S. 𝄋 to Fine

Used In The Motion Picture "2001: A SPACE ODYSSEY"

Also Sprach Zarathustra

Composed by
RICHARD STRAUSS
Arranged by Richard Bradley

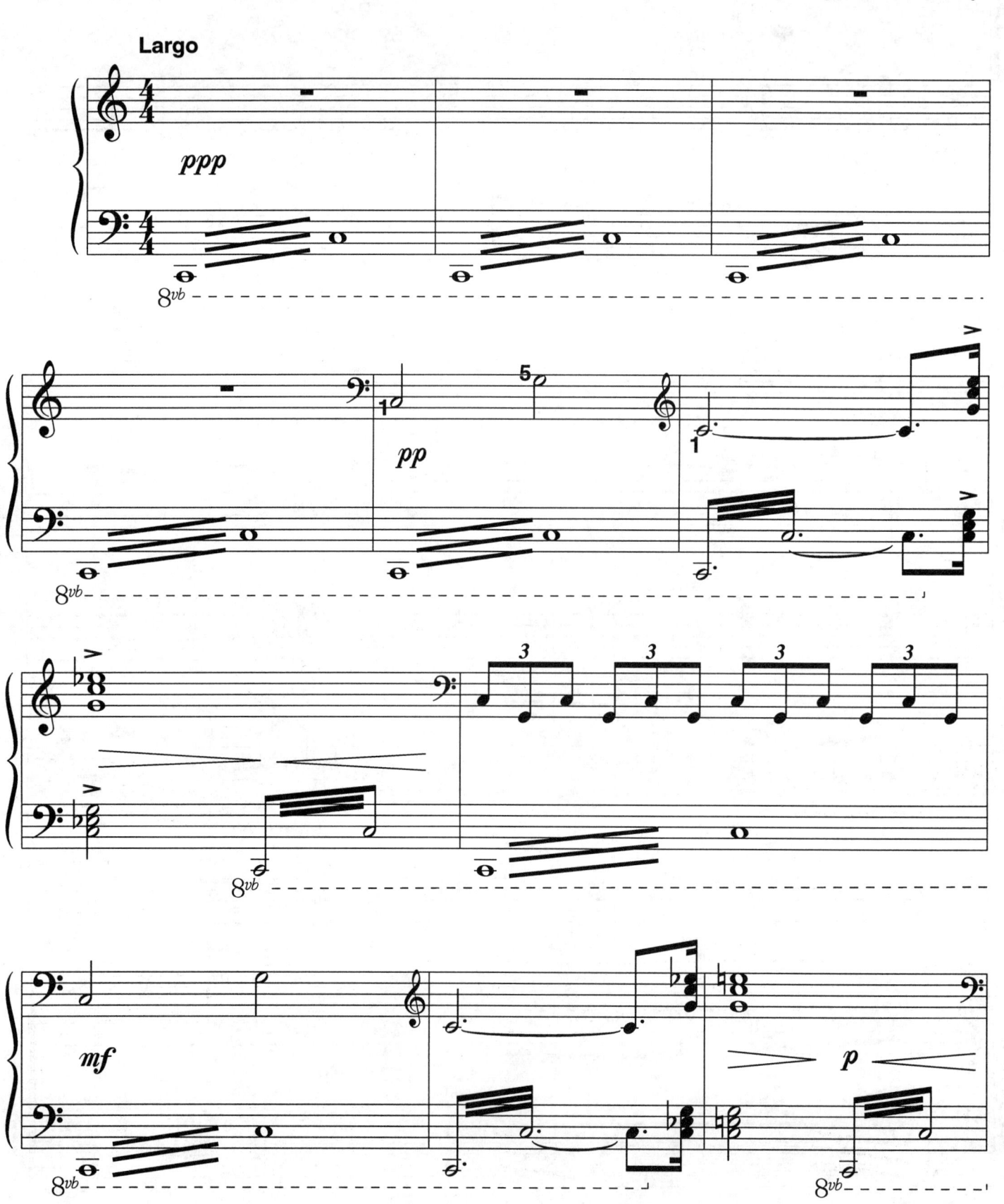

Also Sprach Zarathustra - 2 - 1

Copyright © 1981, 1994 BRADLEY PUBLICATIONS
All Rights Assigned to and Controlled by BEAM ME UP MUSIC (ASCAP), c/o CPP/BELWIN, INC.
15800 N.W. 48th Avenue, Miami, FL 33014
International Copyright Secured   Made in U.S.A.   All Rights Reserved

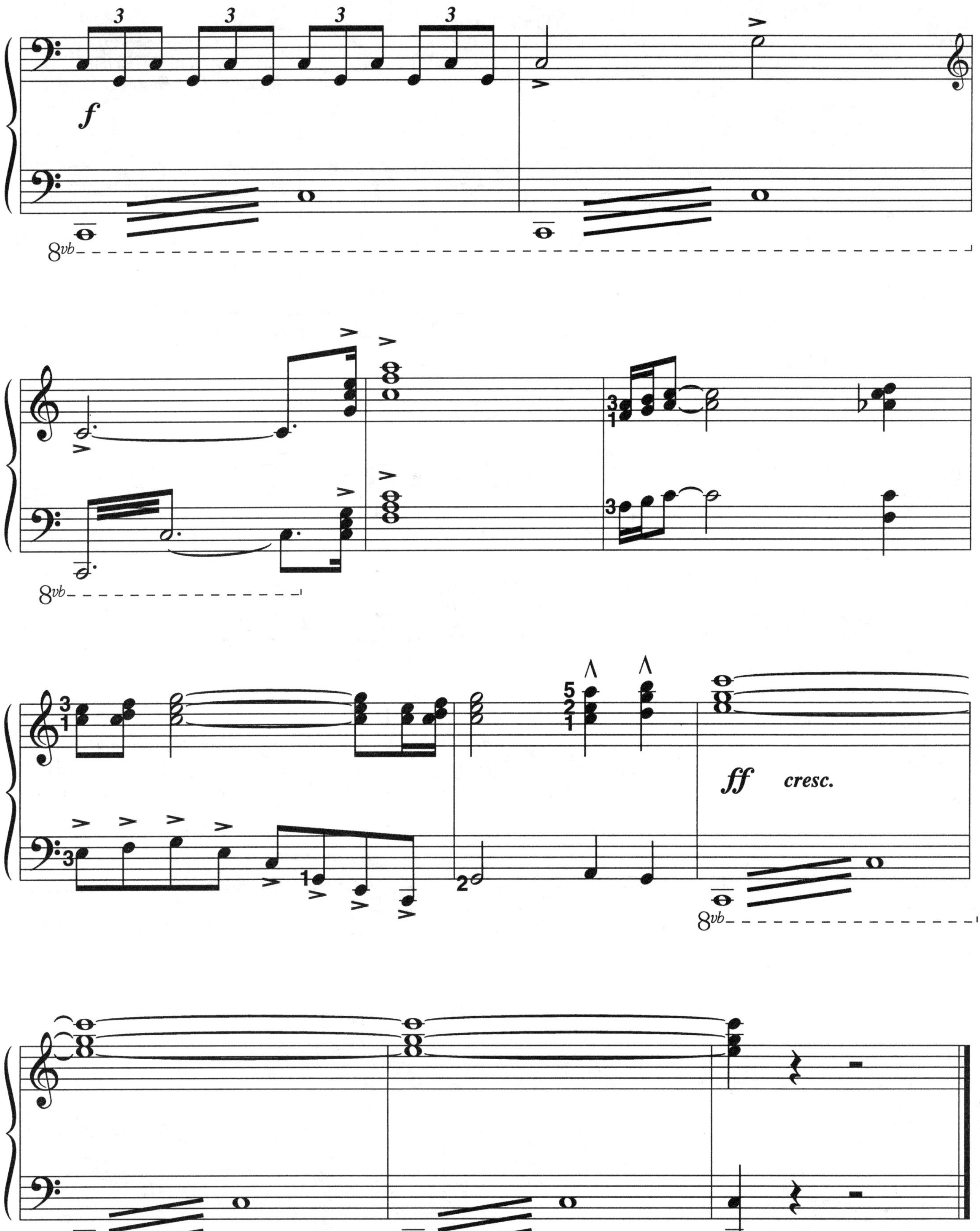
f
8vb
ff
cresc.

Clair de Lune

(First Theme)

Composed by
CLAUDE DEBUSSY
Arranged by Richard Bradley

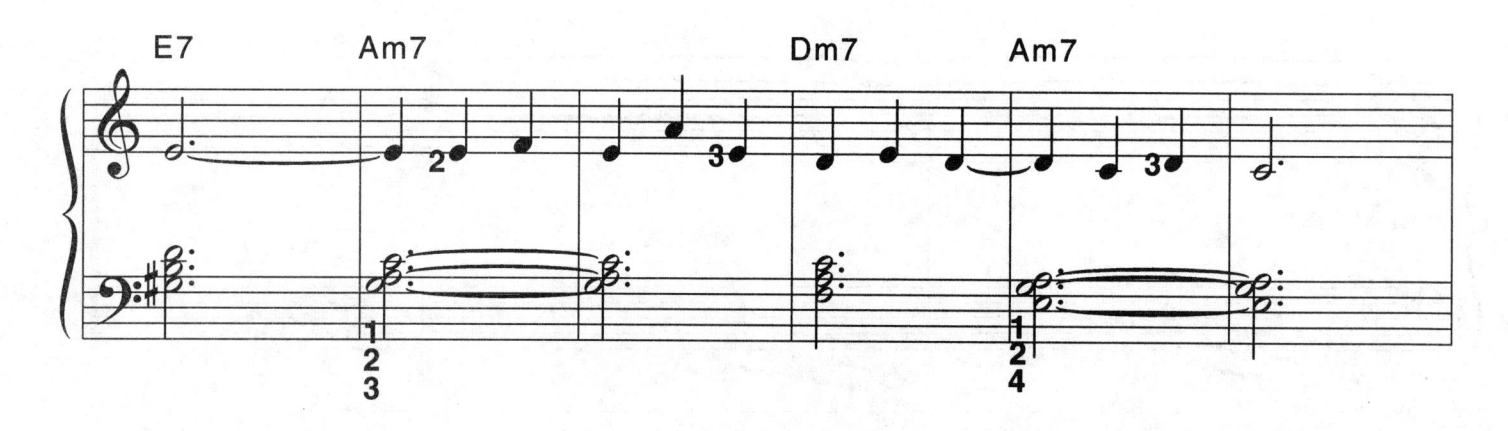

Andante

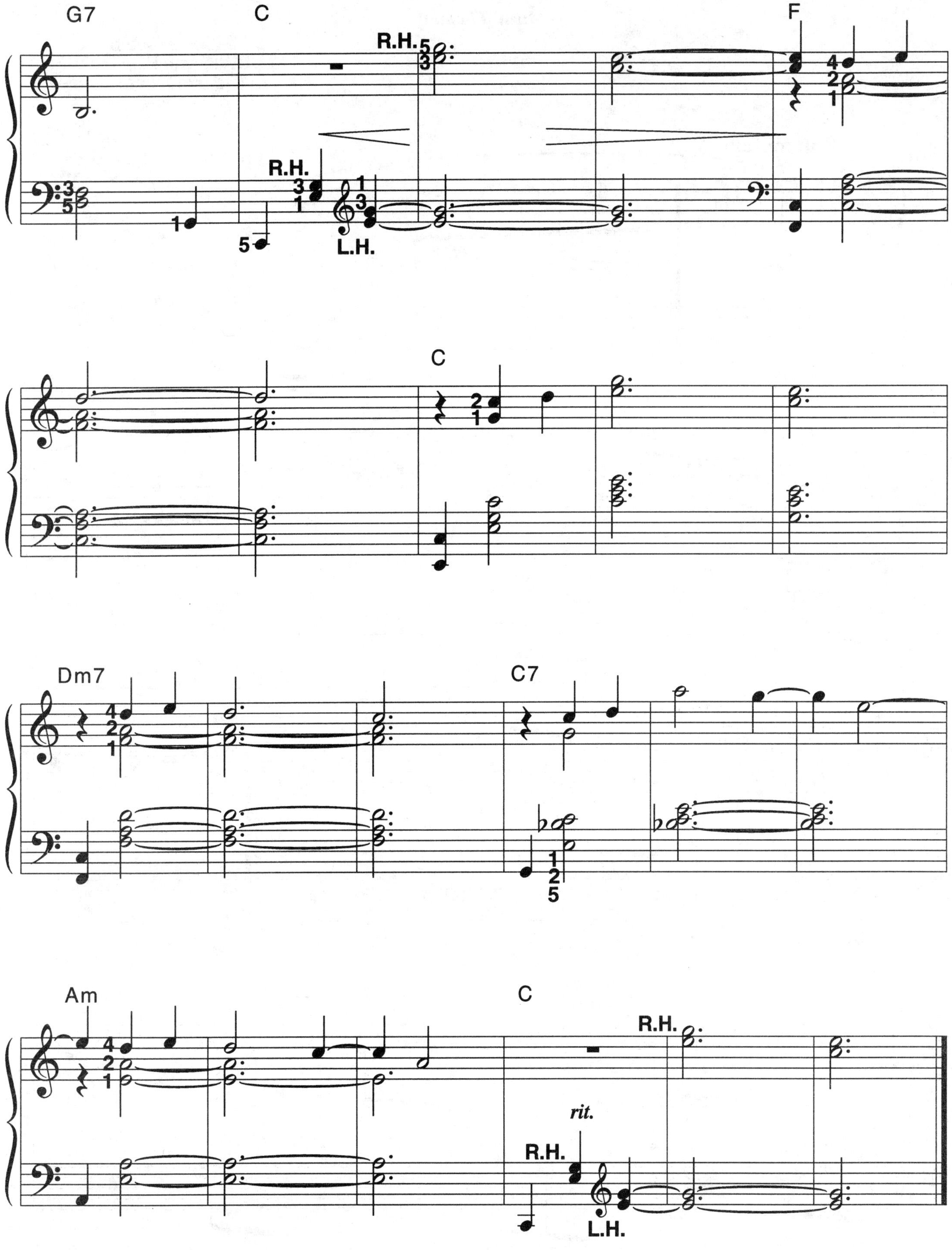
G7
C
R.H.
L.H.
F
C
Dm7
C7
Am
C
R.H.
rit.
R.H.
L.H.

Für Elise

(Main Theme)

Composed by
LUDWIG van BEETHOVEN
Edited by Richard Bradley

75

Canon In D

Composed by
JOHANN PACHELBEL
Arranged by Richard Bradley

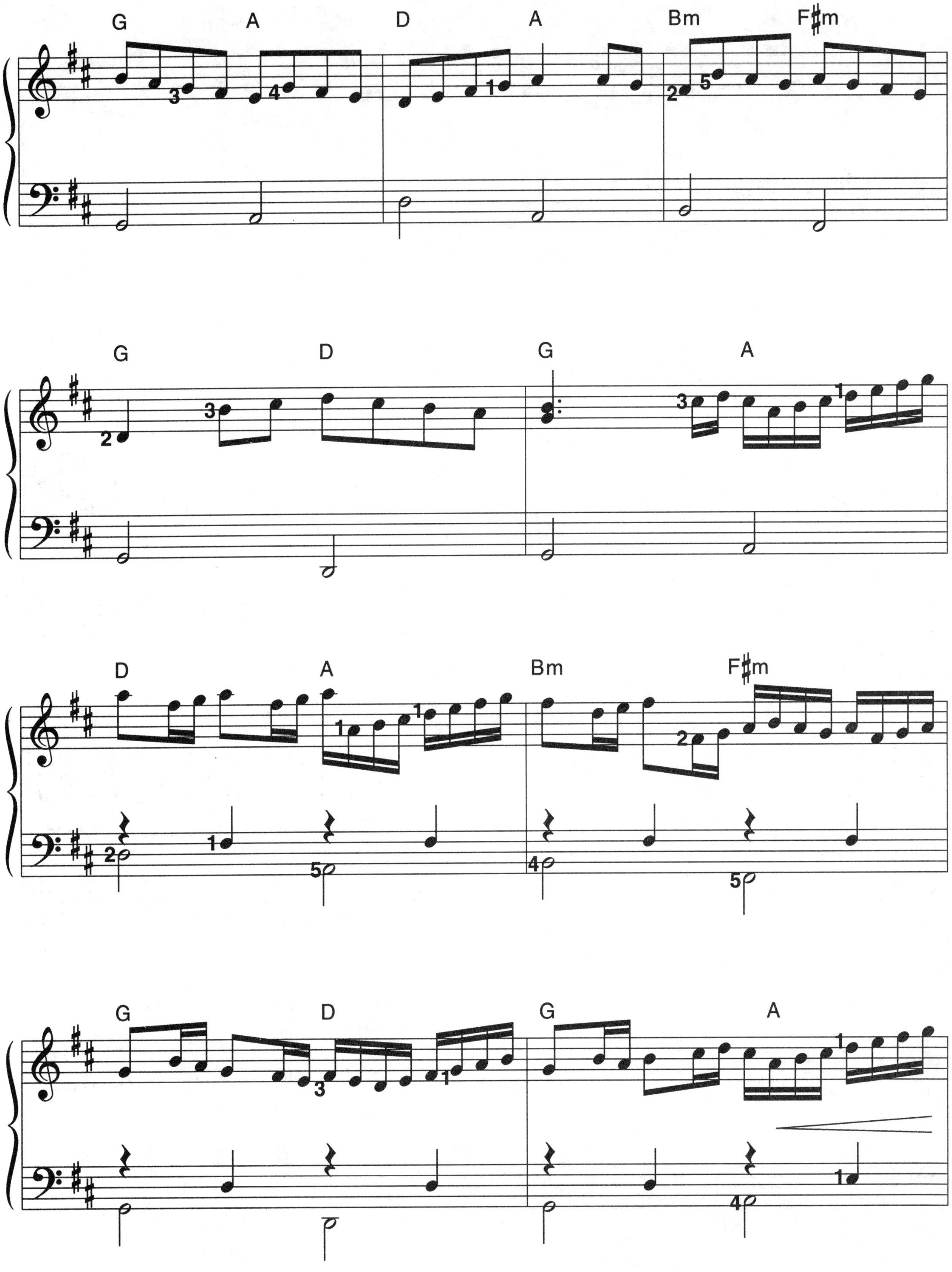
G A D A Bm F♯m
G D G A
D A Bm F♯m
G D G A

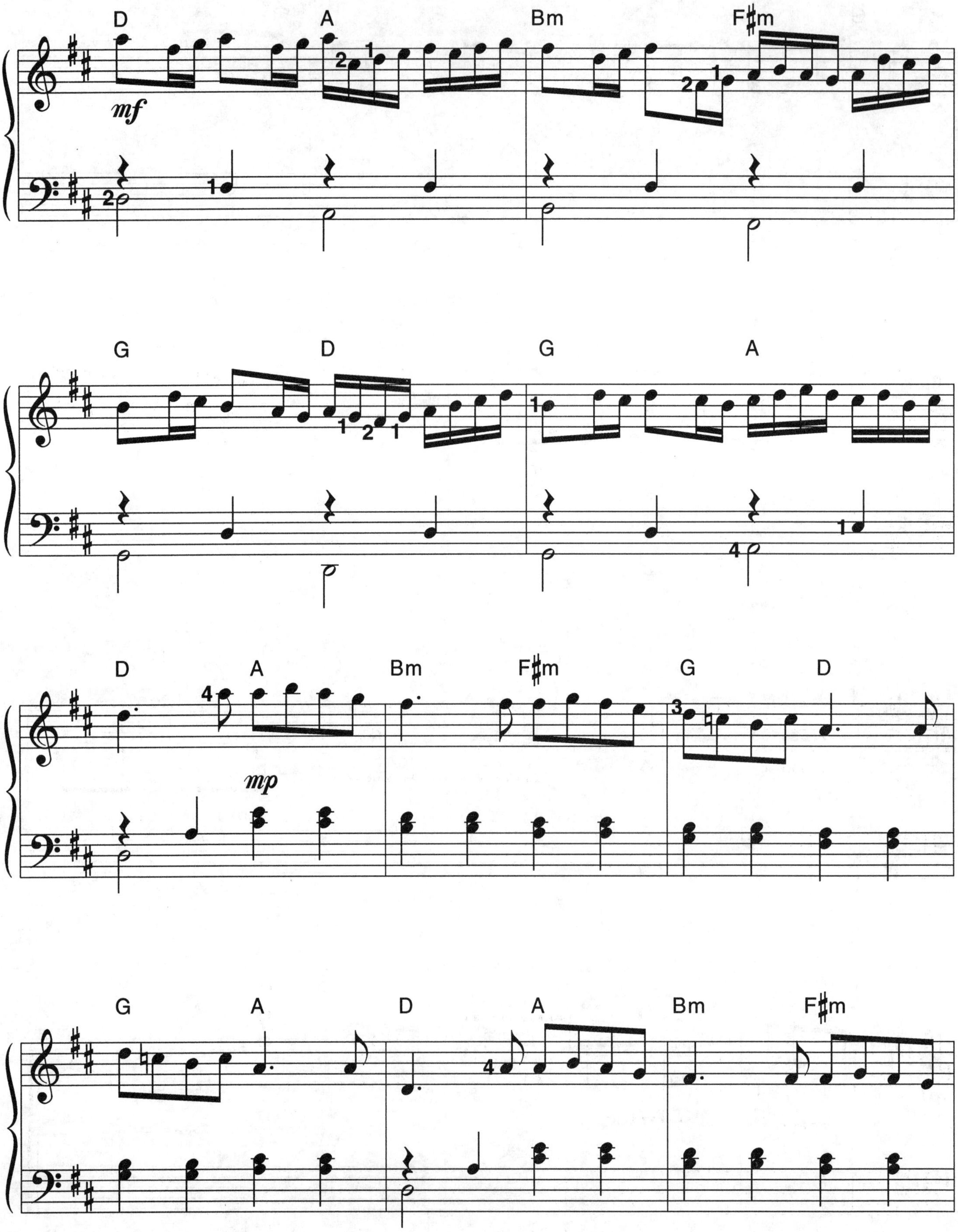
D A Bm F♯m
mf
G D G A
D A Bm F♯m G D
mp
G A D A Bm F♯m

Canon in D - 4 - 4

Misty

Lyric by JOHNNY BURKE

Music by ERROLL GARNER
Arranged by Richard Bradley

2.
F Ab G Gb F NC
near. You can say that you're
cresc.
Cm7 F7
lead - ing me on, but it's just what I
mf
BbMaj7 Cm7 Dm7 NC
want you to do, Don't you no - tice how
Bm7 E7 G7add6
hope - less - ly I'm lost, that's why I'm fol - low - ing

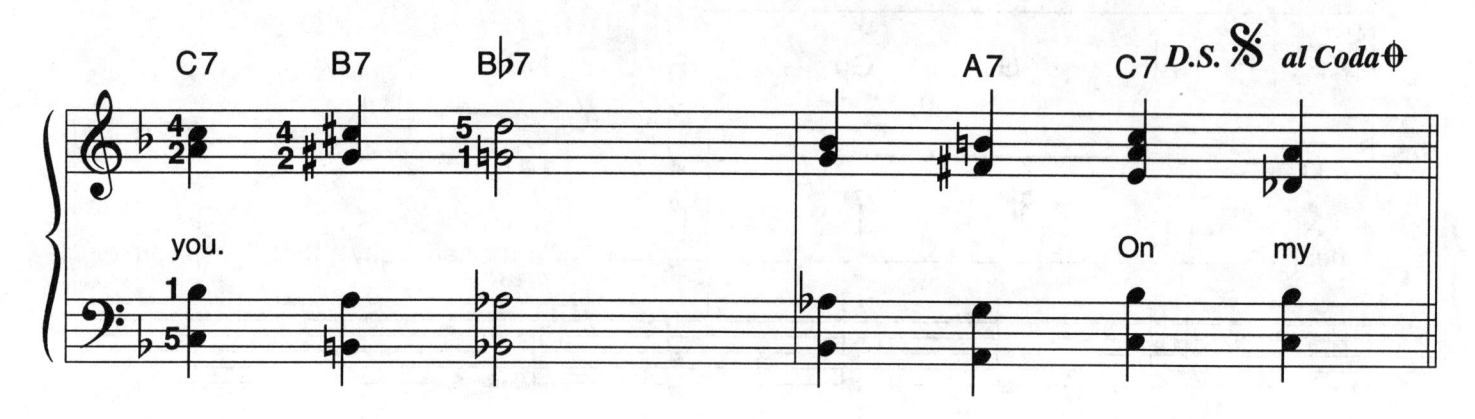

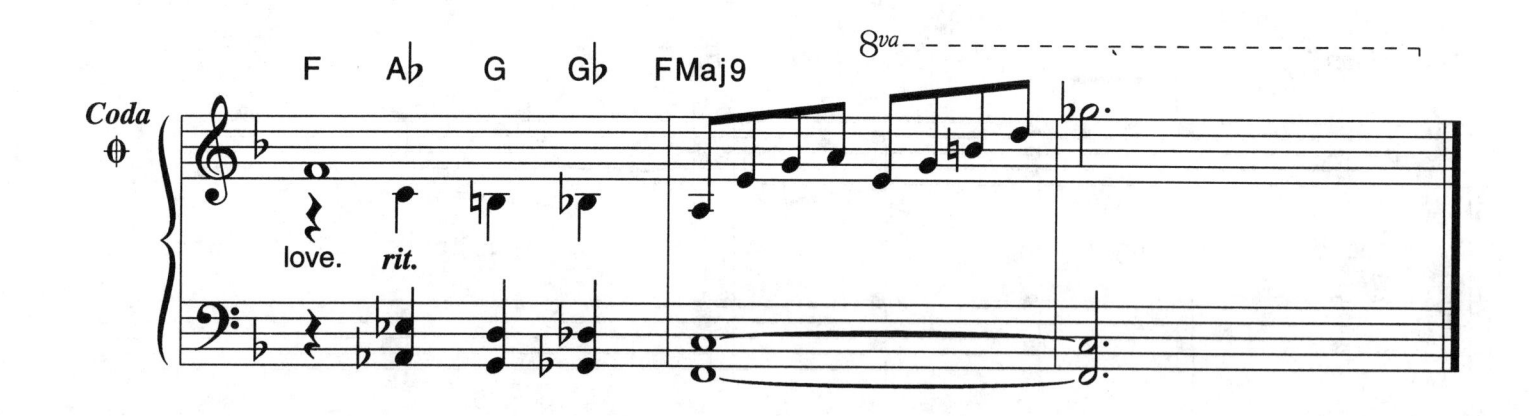

Verse 2:
Walk my way, and a thousand violins begin to play,
Or it might be the sound of your hello,
That music I hear, I get misty the moment you're near.

Verse3:
On my own, would I wander through this wonderland alone,
Never knowing my right foot from my left,
My hat from my glove, I'm too misty and too much in love.

Lullaby Of Birdland

Words by
GEORGE DAVID WEISS

Music by
GEORGE SHEARING
Arranged by Richard Bradley

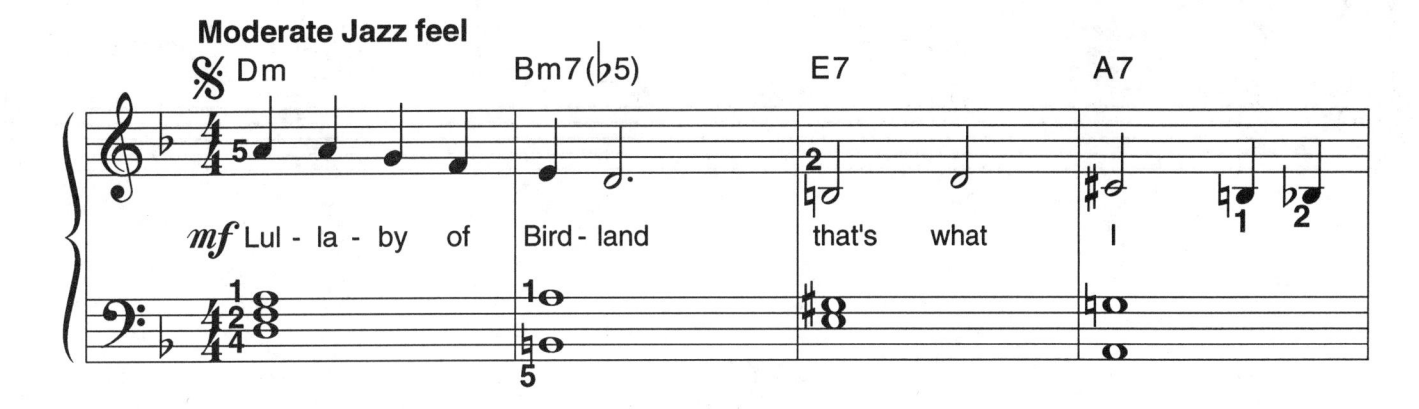

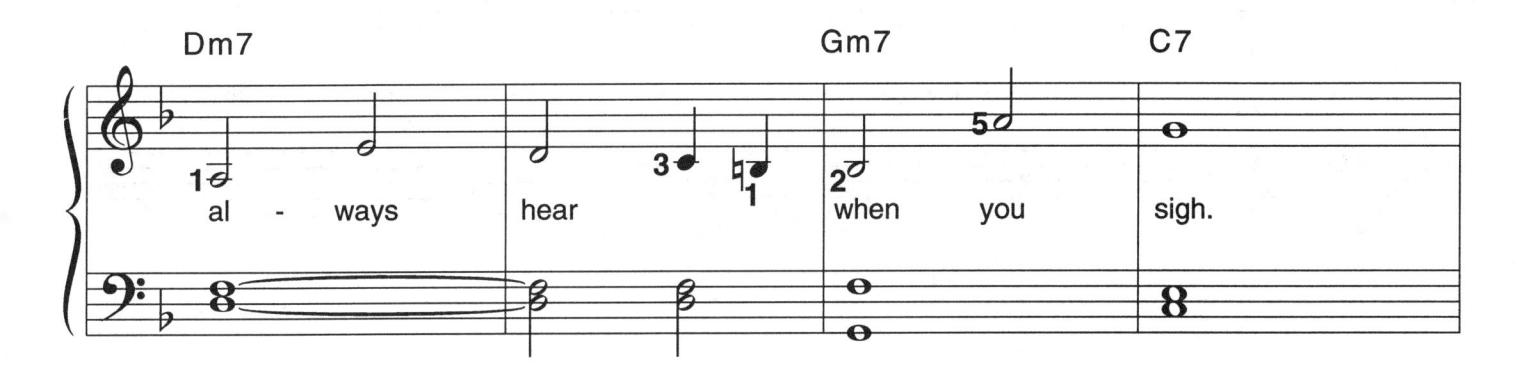

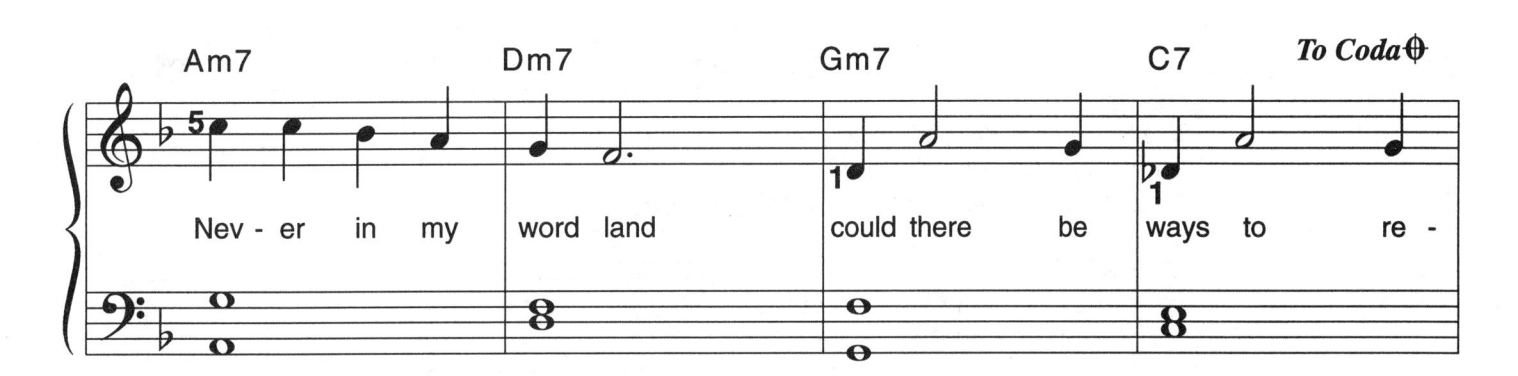

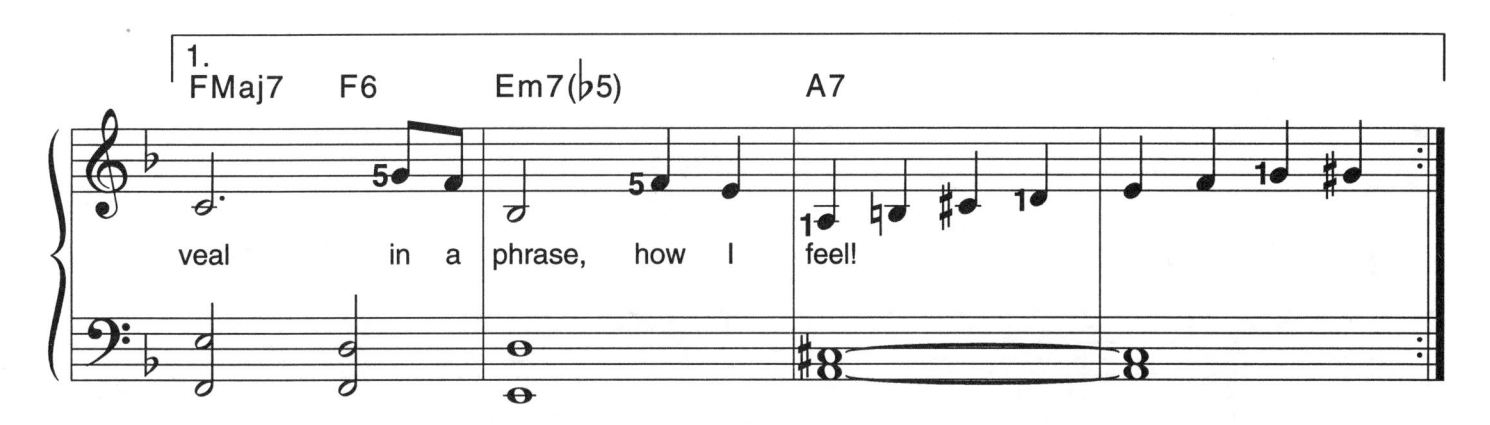

Moderate Jazz feel

mf Lul - la - by of Bird - land that's what I

al - ways hear when you sigh.

Nev - er in my word land could there be ways to re-

1.
veal in a phrase, how I feel!

Lullaby Of Birdland - 3 - 1

Copyright © 1952, 1953, 1954 ADAM R. LEVY & FATHER ENT. INC., 1790 Broadway, New York, NY 10019
This arrangement Copyright © 1986 ADAM R. LEVY & FATHER ENT. INC.
International Copyright Secured   Made in U.S.A.   All Rights Reserved

2.
FMaj7 F6 NC Am7
lips when we kiss! And there's a
D7 NC Gm7 C7 Gm7
weep - y old wil - low; he real - ly
C7 NC FMaj7 F6 Am7
knows how to cry! That's how I'd
D7 NC Gm7 C7 Gm7
cry in my pil - low if you should

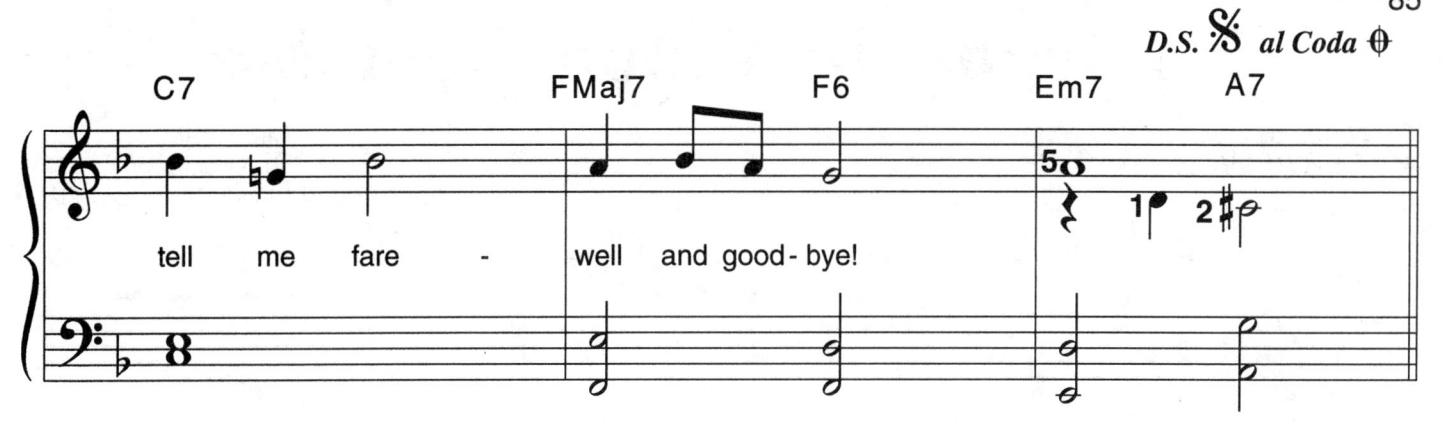

Verse 2:
Have you ever heard two turtle doves
Bill and coo, when they love?
That's the kind of magic music
We make with our lips
When we kiss.

Verse 3:
Lulllaby of Birdland, whisper low,
Kiss me sweet and we'll go
Flyin' high in Birdland,
High in the sky up above
All because we're in love.

Someone To Watch Over Me

Words by
IRA GERSHWIN

Music by
GEORGE GERSHWIN
Arranged by Richard Bradley

C/G
Cdim/G♭
G7/F
Gdim/E
Dm7
I know I could al - ways be good to one who'll
G7(♭9)
C
Cdim
C
watch o - ver me. Al - though he
Fdim
F/C
Fdim
F/C
F
Fm
may not be the man some girls think of as
mf
C/E
F♯m7(♭5)
B7
E7
hand - some. To my heart he car - ries the

A9 D+ G9 G7(♭9) C
key. Won't you tell him please to
F/A Fdim/A♭ C/G Cdim/G♭
put on some speed, fol - low my lead,
G7/F Gdim/E Dm7
oh, how I need some - one to
G7(♭9) CMaj9
watch o - ver me. rit.

The Man I Love

Words by
IRA GERSHWIN

Muisc by
GEORGE GERSHWIN
Arranged by Richard Bradley

Cm
Em7(♭5)/B♭
I'll un - der - stand,
and in a lit - tle while
A7
Dm7(♭5)/A♭
he'll take my hand;
and though it seems ab - surd,
G7
C
Dm
C
Bm7
E7
I know we both won't
say a
word.
Am7
C/E
Cdim/E♭
Dm7
C
Bm7
May - be I shall meet him
Sun - day, may - be
Mon - day may - be
mf
E7
Am7
C/E
Cdim/E♭
Dm7
not;
Still I'm sure to meet him
one day, may - be

91

Embraceable You

Words by
IRA GERSHWIN

Music by
GEORGE GERSHWIN
Arranged by Richard Bradley

Em - brace me, my sweet em - brace - a - ble you! Em - brace me, you ir - re - place - a - ble you! Just one look at you, my heart grew tip - sy in me; You and you a

I love all the man - y charms a - bout you: a - bove all I want my

D.S. % al Coda
Em A7 Am7 D7
lone bring out the gyp - sy in me!
Coda
Dm7 G7 C F♯m7 B7
arms a - bout you. Don't be a naugh - ty ba - by,
Em A9 GMaj7
come to pa - pa, come to pa - pa do! My sweet em -
Am7(♭5) D7 G A♭ GMaj9
brace - a - ble you.
8va
8vb

Strike Up The Band

Words by
IRA GERSHWIN

Music by
GEORGE GERSHWIN
Arranged by Richard Bradley

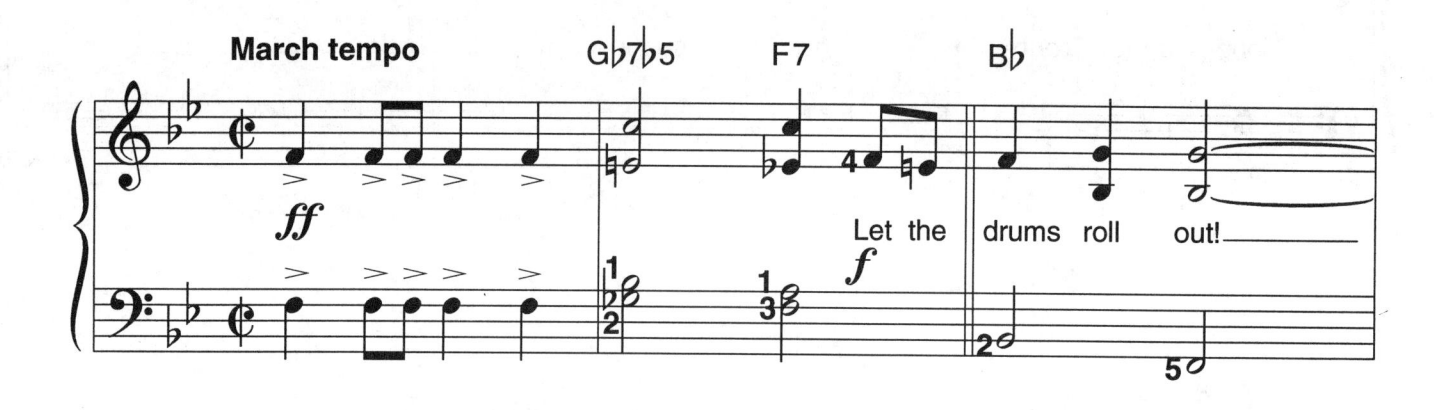

Let the drums roll out! Let the trum-pet call! While the peo-ple shout! Strike up the band! Hear the cym-bals ring! Call-ing

Strike Up The Band - 3 - 1

© 1927 (Renewed) 1986 WB MUSIC CORP.
All Rights Reserved

Edim
B♭
one and all
to the mar - tial swing
E♭
E♭m/B♭
Strike up the band!
There is
B♭
Am
work to be done, to be done! There's a war to be won, to be
D7(♭9)
Gm7
C7
won! Come, you son of a son of a gun! Take your

F7
B♭
stand!
Fall in line, yea bo!
Bdim
Come a - long, Let's go!
Cm7
F7
B♭
B/B♭
Hey lead - er! Strike up the band!
ff
B♭
B/B♭
B♭
B/B♭
B♭
B/B♭
B♭